"Good health has many dimensions—a healthy body, a healthy mind, *and* a healthy spirit that consciously participates with the abundant possibilities beyond the everyday mind. In this intensely entertaining and insightful memoir, Jonna Rae Bartges shares her experiences of those possibilities, and then shows how *everyone* (including you!) has the natural ability to enjoy the psychic and intuitive side of life. *Do* try this at home!"

Bill Gottlieb

Author of *Alternative Cures, Breakthroughs in Drug-Free Healing* and *Speed Healing;* former editor-in-chief, Rodale Books; Prevention Magazine Books

"This profound, moving and often funny metaphysical memoir is a must read for all who gravitate to the magic and mystery of the unseen worlds. Not suggested for skeptics as it will most likely make a believer out of you!"

Arielle Ford

Author of *The Soulmate Secret: Manifest the Love of your Life with the Law of Attraction*; www.soulmatekit.com

"It is so natural to think, 'I know this sounds crazy, but...' Yet that in fact is the true signature of spiritual connection. Because it is so 'out of the ordinary' with no logical explanation, the knee jerk reaction is to deny our psychic truth. Through sharing her own psychic journey extraordinaire, Jonna Rae lights the path we can all follow in our pursuit of the spiritual wonder that will transform our lives."

Dr. Jane Greer

Psychotherapist, author of *The Afterlife Connection: A Therapist Reveal How To Communicate With Departed Loved Ones;* Modera⁺ ⸱ ⸱ "D⸱⸱⸱⸱ ⸱⸱ C⸱⸱ ⸱⸱ b⸱⸱⸱⸱⸱althylife.net

D0916386

"What does psychology have to do with Spirit? Everything. The word 'psychology' comes from the Greek words 'psyche,' meaning 'soul' and 'logos,' meaning 'to speak.' So psychology is literally 'to speak about the soul.' And that is just what Jonna Rae does in her enlightening book—she speaks to our soul. We must realize the mind is the energy source though which the soul expresses itself. We live during a time when we've seen a quantum leap in the field of human consciousness, a time when our interior sense of self is radically changing. Jonna Rae invites us to look at life intuitively—to trust our innate spirituality—and to become partners with our body-mind-spirit for a truly extraordinary life."

Dr. Kay Sudekum Trotter
Licensed Professional Counselor;
Creator of Equine Partners in Counseling (EPIC)

"There is magic in Jonna Rae's book, *Psychic or Psychotic?* I started reading it one morning and couldn't put it down until turning the last page. In a world that seems to be in such a hurry, Jonna Rae suggests that we take a closer look at our journey so that we could really experience all the gifts that surround us. Her stories are full of comfort and hope, and in many ways, she reminds us of that which we may have felt, but were too afraid to accept—that life is a journey, which never ends, and that life is meant for living, not just existing. Thank you, Jonna Rae, for sharing your wisdom."

John Harricharan
International speaker and award-winning author
of the best-seller, *When You Can Walk on Water, Take the Boat*

"In telling us her life story, Jonna Rae tells us about ourselves. There is something in this book for every one of us. Read it and learn, heal, grow—Jonna Rae helps us remember how to enjoy the ride."

Carol Kramer
Former editor of *Body, Mind & Spirit* magazine

PSYCHIC
OR PSYCHOTIC?

Jonna Rae Bartges is co-author of

Gut Feeling: Creating a Healthy Balance in the Ileocecal Valve

Kenny's Journals: The True Story of a Love-Driven Life

PSYCHIC
OR PSYCHOTIC?

MEMOIRS OF A HAPPY MEDIUM
JONNA RAE BARTGES

Copyright © 2010 by Jonna Rae Bartges

Sandra Matuschka: Editor
John Marcum: Designer
Amara Whitham: Illustrator
Max Poppers: Photographer

ISBN 0-7414-6062-9

Printed in the United States of America

Published June 2010

INFINITY PUBLISHING
1094 New DeHaven Street, Suite 100
West Conshohocken, PA 19428-2713
Toll-free (877) BUY BOOK
Local Phone (610) 941-9999
Fax (610) 941-9959
Info@buybooksontheweb.com
www.buybooksontheweb.com

For my husband Paul and little brother Jeffrey,
who both completed their life missions way too early;
also for my friends, in all realms,
who support and encourage this work.

"One thing I know; the only ones among you
who will be really happy
are those who have sought and found how to serve."

--**Albert Schweitzer**

All Purpose Affirmation

I am surrounded in the pure white light
Of the Creator
For love, guidance and protection.
Only good shall come to me,
Only good shall go from me.
I give thanks,
I give thanks,
I give thanks.

Acknowledgments

In my first half-century, my adventures have taken me literally across the country and around the world. I've met, learned from, taught, challenged, been challenged by and loved some spectacular people, all of whom helped create this book. I want to thank my parents and two brothers, who gave me the opportunity to learn independence and self-confidence before spreading my wings.

Thanks to the brilliant mind of John Marcum for his cover and interior design work; Amara Whitham for her original painting gracing the back cover and illustrating a transformational dream vision; Max Poppers for his cover, author and Practical Spirituality 101 class photography and Sandi Matuschka for her fantastic and intuitively right-on editing prowess.

Some teachers who profoundly influenced me and stayed in my heart are Virginia Samdahl, Elizabeth Reed, Elizabeth Trainer, Joan Laudenslager, Beatrice Stone, Frances Bixler and Willard Lally. Tuned-in bosses have included Greg Albrecht, Celeste Lanuza, Lindsay Schnebly, Roy Heffelfinger, Alex Rozsa, Bill Thomas and Jim Paratore.

For friendship and/or inspiration: thanks to Dr. Rhonda Honeycutt, Elma Broadfoot, Brenda Gerhard, Kathy Echroll, Dr. Jan Berlin, Pam Espinosa, Dr. Kay Trotter, Dr. Jane Greer, Whit Neblett, Erin Raskin, Coni Rosati, Charmiene Maxwell-Batten, Dr. Tom Reidarson, Jim Antrim, Dr. Jim McBain, Revs. Dr. Jeni and Rick Prigmore, Wendy Nethersole, Jay Whitham, Fuzzman, Dharma, Minerva, Bear, Patrick Alo, Kelle Olwyler, Max Poppers, Julie Parker, Sandi Tomlin-Sutker, Spiritsong, Selina DeLangre, Dr. Charley Scott, Dr. Jennifer Oliver Liming, Arielle Ford,

Sparrow, Cecilia Flores, Kathi and Sheldon Butler, Bill Gottlieb, Dr. Ann Weber, Diane English, Diane Burris, Darla Adams, Jim Goure, Carol Lyons, George Clooney, Jon Stewart, Bono, Oprah and Walt Disney.

Table of Contents

Introduction

When my dear husband Paul was dying from metastasized melanoma in 2001, I received a powerful dream vision. He and I were standing on a mountaintop, hand in hand. Together we gazed into the distance toward the west, where another mountaintop was barely visible through the mist that enshrouded it. Between the two mountains was a huge chasm, so deep no bottom was visible from our lofty perch.

As I observed myself in the dream, I kissed Paul, and then started constructing a winding bridge from our peak to the distant one. I was manifesting cobblestones to create a path, and I knew intuitively that each of the stones represented a tear, or a significant life lesson. It was definitely a spirit bridge; although there was no visible supporting structure, it was wide and sturdy, and created a permanent link from where we were, to the other side.

I knew that when I finished building this bridge, Paul would cross over, and die. I also knew a huge group of people would soon follow him.

The other thing that was clear to me was that the bridge was not just to guide the dying safely into the next world, but to allow those of us in physical bodies to cross more easily back and forth between spirit and form. I accepted the huge responsibility of creating this connection with humility and gratitude.

I shared the vision with Paul, and it gave him great peace. He made the journey in February 2001; seven months later, on September 11, that bridge was packed with transitioning souls.

I also shared the vision with my little brother Jeffrey, an attorney in private practice in Emmaus, Pennsylvania. He was the only member of the family with whom I could freely talk about my psychic experiences, and through the decades, we shared everything that was in our hearts. He said how sorry he'd been that Dad made it so tough on me with his sarcasm and constant ridicule of anything smacking of the metaphysical.

The way I'd finally come to deal with it, I told Jeff, was accepting the concept that we actually choose our parents to help us learn specific lessons on our life path. By experiencing a difficult childhood, I definitely developed my independent streak at an early age. To deflect and defuse tense confrontations, I also developed a wild sense of humor.

That humor has been my saving grace growing up psychic. It got me through college, when my classmates, and some professors, were afraid of the things I was able to do. It cloaked me during my spiritual quest in my 20s, when I left the real world to discover once and for all if I was "psychic" or "psychotic." It helped me survive bad relationships, demanding jobs for global corporations like Disney and Sea World, the harsh judgments of others and feeling the emotions of people, situations—even the planet—on a sometimes overwhelming soul level.

My humor also helped me survive some heart-breaking deaths—Paul's, Jeffrey's in 2008, and my own near-death experience from a cerebral aneurysm back in 1989. I astonished my neurosurgeon by joking with him I knew it was "all in my head."

Because my sense of humor has always been at the heart of how I live, I adopted the name "Happy Medium Jonna Rae" as my persona for spiritual consulting and teaching work. Although the information I see, hear, and feel for clients is very serious, delivering it with respect and joy makes it so much easier for people to accept, and use in a positive way. In fact my slogan is, "I see dead people so you don't have to."

Even before the bridge vision, I felt called to help people acknowledge and develop their own natural psychic abilities so they could enrich their lives on all levels. In a deep meditation back in 1979, I was shown how to guide people to their inner awareness, and I've been teaching "Practical Spirituality 101" ever since. I warn students they're not getting out of the room until they can do an accurate reading, and it always works. I also use humor to help people accept this very powerful, frequently repressed part of themselves. Usually I start the two-day class by saying, "How many of you believe in telekinesis? Raise my hand...."

For years, people have been telling me I needed to write a book about my life. I've hesitated to step into that spotlight, and prayed for some kind of sign. Then, I found it.

I was looking for a photo in some computer files I hadn't opened in years, and was thrilled to discover a big collection of Jeff's old e-mails. Here's an excerpt from the first note I opened, one he'd sent back in 2001:

You mentioned about a year ago that you had a powerful image of a bridge...you shared with me your vision of crossing the bridge, showing others the way over the bridge, of 'being' the bridge, and understanding for the first time all the little cobblestones. I will forever think of that when I think of you. You have a wonderful combination of a sensitivity to the eternal and spiritual, and a delightful understanding of human nature and what makes us mere humans think, find joy, be happy, and learn. Few people are blessed as you to have a solid footing in both worlds. And, you show others the way. You point to the bridge. I am still squinting into the fog shrouding the bridge wondering if I have the courage to set foot on it. You go, girl. Embrace that. You're a Gemini, for goodness sake...it should be natural.

Get out that spotlight and fog horn and show people that bridge. That's what you are to do. You are a guide and a teacher and a healer and you have endured the painful fires of purification and are finding your voice. I just feel it. I lift you up in prayer and send the feeble rays of light I can gather and send your way. I love you so much. You are on to the truth that our relationship with God is the one constant in our lives. 'I believe what I believe is what makes me what I am,' a song says. 'Let me grasp for the light, which is out of reach and die en route to a star,' a poem says. Be that bridge to light and stars and faith and love. I'm counting on you.

We love you so much.—BLB

A quick note here—Jeff's "BLB" signature stood for "Bratty Little Brother," part of our affectionate sibling code for each other. I was "WBS"—Wonderful Big Sister.

But gently refocusing…. Finding Jeff's directive to "Show people that bridge!" was the message I was waiting for to create this book. The same way I fit the cobblestones together to make that winding bridge, I'll be fitting together little vignettes that tell my life story to expand your own awareness of what's possible.

Writing this book has definitely taken me outside my comfort zone. It's made me realize, though, that until people can speak openly about how their natural intuitive ability is an important part of their daily lives, too many others will continue to repress and deny this aspect of who they truly are. Even worse, they'll ridicule others or discipline children who start to exercise their own sensitivity. That simply cannot continue to be the norm.

By sharing these vignettes from my life, my intent is that others will recognize some of their own similar experiences for what they are—examples of what happens when they trust and use this natural intuitive ability that everyone has.

My intention with these pages is to bridge the gap between the psychic and the "accepted" normal; between the living and the spirit worlds; between religious judgment and compassion, and between science and spirituality. The time has come to focus on all the things we have in common globally when we have the courage to expand beyond our comfort zones.

It's definitely time to reach a happy medium! Let's cross that bridge together now.

Hugs!

Jonna Rae

Chapter 1

Oh, Yeah. I Died Once.

The dying part was easy. It was deciding to come back and continue living my life that was the real challenge.

I floated between worlds, watching my motionless body lying empty on the bed. Then my spirit dipped back into my physical form only to be overwhelmed by the searing pain ripping through my head. Violent convulsions gagged me, robbing my lungs of precious air. My legs defied my brain's command to move. Besides the obvious physical detractors of electing to stay in my body, emotionally I didn't feel a strong desire to hang around, either.

For three challenging years before this current moment suspended between life and death, I was slowly losing all my vital life force in a very bad marriage. I had tried on a dream that just didn't fit. My then-husband, let's call him "Ed," was the spitting image of my dad—belligerent, follicle-challenged, sarcastic, judgmental, critical of my weight despite his own jowly paunchiness, and cruelly dismissive of my psychic abilities. Dismissive? Let's turn that up a few notches. Just like Dad, he openly ridiculed my sensitivity to the point where I decided it was easier to keep it undercover, just as I did when I still lived at home back in Allentown, Pennsylvania, half a continent away.

Now, though, I was doing the dance of deflection in a whole new setting. Ed was the general manager of a group of television stations in Kansas, I was the creative services director, and we'd built a lovely home in Wichita. We had met working together at a TV station in Miami. I was the Emmy® and Addy®-award winning advertising and promotions manager, and he had come in as the new news director. I'd arrived in Miami by way of Asheville, North Carolina, the last spot on my two-year spiritual quest to find out if I was psychic or psychotic. I'd learned—and received confirmation from friends who just happened to be psychologists—that I definitely wasn't nuts. Occasionally over-dramatic, silly, impulsive, impatient and extremely creative, *yes*—but certifiably mentally unstable? Nope. When I was told in meditation to teach my spiritual truths by living them, and to get back into the real world, I ended up becoming executive news producer at WLOS, the ABC affiliate in Asheville. More about that later.

If I'm so darn psychic, one might ask, just why did I marry this guy in the first place? Psychology 101—I was still dealing with childhood issues of wanting a father's approval and love. No matter how intuitive we are, the basic hurts are still the same. Besides, Ed was very intelligent, and he said all the right things, like, he was going to change his personality completely, and I was the perfect woman to help him do it.

Despite all the red flags such a sweeping and unrealistic claim unfurled, I *so* wanted to believe him. So, I blissfully ignored the warnings of my friends in both the real and spirit worlds, and said, "I do." And I tried. I did.

Who You Gonna Call?

The inconvenient truth of this marriage was I came to believe Ed, 14 years my senior, married me so he'd have someone to take care of him when he became old and incapacitated, just as his mom took care of his dad. At the same time, on another dimension, he was effectively helping me confront the "dad" issues of being ridiculed as a kid. Ed was sarcastic, controlling, and judgmental—exactly the male dynamic with which I was familiar. He was the perfect person to help me finally recognize and heal these old wounds. But first, of course, we had to dance a bit.

I would "see" flashing red warning lights all around him. Occasionally his insensitivity and cruelty would reduce me to tears. Just about everyone tried to talk me out of marrying this guy, and pointed out we had NOTHING in common other than both being carbon-based life forms. I kept trying to convince myself that all the major personality changes he said he was going to make, he would. How eager we all are to embrace a good fantasy when the reality of the situation leaves much to be desired! Even now, I can hear the roar of laughter from my angel guides....

Instead of boring you with all the little indicators that this union was NOT a good thing, I want to share one particular dramatic event that was literally right out of the *Ghostbusters* movies. Remember those slimy neon green negative spirits the busters battled? That stuff is all real.

One night I awoke to see that exact image—the very same neon green blobby horrid creature, floating just above Ed. I strongly felt it was an extension of him, connected to him on an energetic level, and directed by Ed's deepest inner core. As I stared, shocked, at the apparition, it started slowly to ooze toward me, extending slimy arms in my direction, twisting its top third into a menacing face.

I tightly shut my eyes and began fervidly whispering my all-purpose affirmation, surrounding myself in strong Christ light. When I opened my eyes, the creature was gone. My trepidation, though, and my growing awareness that this marriage was a disaster, were both just starting to gear up.

Hallway Centurions

Another vivid memory of how Ed and I were pretty much on different planets in every respect, particularly the psychic, happened during a business trip to England. Our little Kansas group was enjoying a lovely dinner in the dining hall of our sprawling hotel, and I started to feel a bit of a draft.

"I'm just going to run up to the room and grab a sweater," I told Ed.

Whether it was a conscious effort to save on energy costs, or an intentionally dramatic effect, the centuries-old building did not have an abundance of lights in the wide hallways. Being sensitive, I've always had good radar for feeling activity on other dimensions, and I was getting major goose bumps as I ran up the dimly illuminated carpeted staircase to the next floor.

Just as I turned into the corridor that ran in front of our room, I stopped. A ghostly regimen of Roman centurions, clad for battle and in perfect lockstep, marched silently through the shadowy expanse of the hallway, directly toward me. I spun around and flew back down the stairs to the dining hall.

"I thought you were cold?" Ed said quizzically as I slid back into my chair, sans that sweater.

"I'm good!" I answered. Somehow, a little draft seemed immensely preferable to having the spectral Roman Legion marching right through me. And, of course, I never bothered to mention anything about my encounter to Ed. I just didn't feel like being ridiculed that evening.

Resurrecting Regis

Brief tangent here—Ed was the general manager of the television station group and decided he didn't like the hugely popular, nationally syndicated talk show, *Regis and Kathie Lee*. Now remember, we're talking the heartland of America. Our viewers loved Regis and Kathie Lee, and considered them personal friends—no, more—family members! I tried to talk him out of canceling it, but he insisted that no one would miss the program, and removed it from the schedule.

Of course, the letters and phone calls started rolling in. The viewers had spoken. They wanted their daily Regis and Kathie Lee. Ed gave me the new job of dreaming up some kind of a promotional campaign to announce that Regis and Kathie Lee were coming back on the schedule, without admitting we'd made a strategic mistake.

Although I wasn't actively talking about my psychic abilities during my marriage to Ed, I was still frequently covertly tapping into them. In this case, I went into deep meditation to try to "see" the perfect solution for the little PR conundrum. And, by golly, I immediately got it.

I wrote the script for a promo, and sent it to the *Regis* producers to get their buyoff. They loved the idea, and agreed to film the script I sent them. The minute I received the raw material back from them, I set to work producing the final version of the promo that our angry viewers would see.

At the beginning of the promotional spot, Regis and Kathie Lee were sitting on their talk show set in their usual chairs, but everything was in black and white. They both had their eyes closed, and they were saying, in unison, "There's no place like Channel 3, there's no place like Channel 3...." My brilliant director did cool sound effects, and added a little ripple to the video. Then there was a "magic" edit that transitioned into a brilliant color image of the two popular co-hosts looking around the set with animated excitement.

"Reege!" Kathy Lee gasped dramatically, "We're back in Kansas!"

"Yes!" Regis delightfully over-acted. "And our little show, too!"

This promotion, which I had seen in meditation and produced exactly as it was shown to me, became such a hit all through the heartland that several viewers wrote in to accuse us of deliberately taking the show off the air for a while just so we could run that promotion.

But now, gently refocusing....

Looking at Options....

As I was saying, the color had pretty much gone from my life, too. Even though I had made some great friends in Kansas, including some I still treasure today, this cruelly restrictive, tightly controlled existence was emotionally abusive—just like my childhood—and definitely not the lifetime for which I felt I had signed up. I was far off my spiritual path, and completely miserable.

But then, I got my own very personal, very intense lesson in the reality of free will. The night of June 26, I had a "dream" that signaled everything was about to change.

I was alone, standing on a beautiful sloping hill. I knew the gently rolling meadow was a graveyard, even though there weren't tombstones jutting up from the lush green grass. My eyes were drawn to a lovely tree, like a cypress, with fingers of sunlight streaming through the needle-tufted branches. The location was peaceful, sacred, and important; a kind of meeting place among dimensions of consciousness and existence.

It reminded me of the divine intimacy of Rumi's poem: "Out beyond the ideas of wrongdoing and rightdoing, there is a field. I'll meet you there."

I understood on a very deep soul level this spot was not of this Earth, and that my being there was monumentally significant. I gazed around the gentle slope, this graveyard, and quietly asked, "Did my father-in-law die?" He was quite ill at the time.

"No," a deep gentle voice answered.

"Did my husband die?"

"No," the voice responded again.

"Did *I* die?" I swallowed hard, awaiting the answer from this unseen spiritual source.

"Maybe you did, and maybe you didn't," the voice said gently. "It's for you to decide. And don't be frightened."

As the enormity of those words began to penetrate every cell of my being, it felt like I was wrapped in huge wings. An unfathomable sense of grace and love and peace began radiating warmth on the top of my head, and slowly enveloped my entire body. I truly feel I touched into the biblical "peace that passeth all understanding." It was at once beautiful, compassionate, tender, powerful, healing, and just pure love. The entire scene faded away in a big spiral of white light, and I was wide awake.

"Ok, God," I said silently. "THAT meant something!" Then I promptly forgot all about it—until my life hung in the balance.

Chapter 2

Houston, We Have a Problem

Two days after that transcendent dream, Ed left early for work and I slowly awoke to an empty house. I was surprised to realize I had a splitting headache. I *never* get headaches. It must have been that swordfish I had the night before, I reasoned, and then started to get out of bed. Imagine my surprise when I discovered I was unable to coordinate any movement in my legs. As I paused to consider this strange state of things, I also began to realize I was having some trouble breathing. On top of that, I was starting to gag repeatedly.

"Oh," I thought to myself, as realization dawned. "This is about that dream! I could die now if I wanted to."

Precisely because of that beautiful, powerful, comforting dream, I felt absolutely no fear the whole time I was realizing that life was starting to leave my body. I understood I had complete control over what was about to happen, or not happen. It was all totally up to me.

Instead of just calling the paramedics, I decided to call Ed's secretary at work. I guess on some level I knew she could simultaneously call for help *and* tell Ed—I didn't have the juice for *two* phone calls. "Grace" immediately picked up her phone, and was very concerned when she heard my garbled speech. "Jonna!" she said. "Are you okay?"

"Grace," I said slowly, clutching the phone to my face and forcing my mouth around the words that seemed to be floating just beyond my reach. "I need you to call the paramedics. I need you to tell them we hid the key to the house under the planter on the patio. I think this is pretty serious."

That was all I could manage to say. My lungs were straining for air…my tongue was a pillowy mass that splayed across my lips. I dropped the phone to the floor.

Enter the Cavalry

As I lay there staring at the ceiling, losing more and more sensation in my legs and starting to involuntarily gag, I realized with some bizarre amusement that what happened next was entirely up to me. I surfed across the waves of pain that were washing through my skull. I followed the jagged struggle of my lungs to capture another breath. I felt the dead weight of my now useless legs. The one thing I did NOT feel, though, was fear.

I stayed in my body, unable to move yet very aware, very present, until I heard the sound of the key turning in the front door lock.

"Where is she?" I heard men's voices yell, and footsteps running in several directions through the house. One pair of footsteps ran into the master bedroom.

"HERE SHE IS!"

The clattering heels converged into the room and a pair of hands grabbed my wrist. Gently, peacefully, gloriously, I let go. I drifted up to the ceiling then paused to watch the navy blue-clad bodies huddling over me.

"THERE'S NO PULSE!"

"WE'RE LOSING HER!"

"GET THAT IV!"

I heard a gurney snapping into place.

"ONE…TWO…THREE!" The team slid me from the bed to the stretcher, barking out orders the entire time.

It was fascinating to watch, particularly because I hadn't officially decided if this was to be my closing act. In minutes, I was loaded into the ambulance, and the crew raced toward the hospital. During the mad dash, I hovered a few feet over my body, observing, reflecting, and deciding. I hated my life with Ed. Did I hate it enough to die? I wasn't completely sure.

My DESTINY

Part of my hesitation to just take the easy way out of a miserably unhappy situation was because of something a psychic had said to me decades before, when I was covering her lecture for the Allentown Morning Call newspaper. Helen Schreiber was a very well known medium in the area, and several hundred people showed up for her presentation. I sat in the middle of the crowd and listened as she shared a few messages from dead relatives. Suddenly she stopped, and walked right over to my section.

"You," she said, pointing to me. I turned my head to the left and right to see to whom she was talking.

"No, YOU!" she said again, a bit impatiently. I pointed to myself and raised my eyebrows in a silent question.

"YES, you! Do you know you're a healer?" Everyone else was staring at me now. "You're an energy healer, and you're also a gifted psychic." I started scribbling down notes. Little chills were going up and down my spine. I was simultaneously terrified and thrilled to be singled out, and equally terrified and thrilled with what she was telling me.

"You're going to do work to raise world consciousness, and you'll really start coming into your power when you're in your 40s." I was only 17—this was a pretty heady prediction to lay on a kid. My apprehension must have shown on my face.

"Don't worry about it," she said. "You'll know what to do." That consciousness-shifting encounter from my youth still resonated in my soul these 18 years later.

As I hovered near the ceiling enthralled with the drama unfolding below, it dawned on me that if Helen was right, I still hadn't fulfilled my destiny this lifetime.

Maybe that quick exit wasn't the best choice right now. Maybe my *real* life was just about to get started. My vacillation was punctuated by the beeps and static-shrouded voices from the paramedics' two-way radios as they communicated with dispatch.

I've always had the greatest respect for emergency crews. My appreciation deepened as I personally experienced their skill, professionalism, speed, and kindness. Even though I still didn't know for sure if I wanted to stay in my body, keeping me in there was the sole objective of the entire team. They were warriors battling the Angel of Death while I continued to flirt with him.

Traipsing Through Dimensions

The ER doctor was waiting for us at the entrance. He had just lost a woman to a brain aneurysm the week before, and from all the information the paramedics had transmitted en route, he was reasonably sure that's what I was experiencing. He was right.

Because I was drifting in and out of my body during this time, some of my memories are crystal clear, and others are shadowy.

One thing I *do* vividly recall was looking at my body in the CAT scan, then floating over to the monitor where the medical team was studying the images.

"There's the bleed, right there," one of them said, pointing to a dark mass on my brain. "That's not good," he added.

I floated closer to get a better look.

A number of people who have had a near-death experience talk about entering a tunnel of white light, and being greeted by friends and relatives in spirit. That was not my personal reality.

I feel that because I was entirely conscious of the fact that I had a decision to make, and because I was actively considering the pros (I get to fly!) and cons (no more Häagen Dazs®!) of crossing over, the incorporeal Welcoming Committee stayed in the periphery. Even when I flat-lined, which I did several times that week, I was conscious of their presence the whole time, and the proximity of the portal to the other side, but I had not yet called either to me.

In retrospect, I realize it was another powerful proof of creating your reality through the things you focus on. I had not yet clarified my intent, so the portal and spirit people stayed in the shadows.

Because the bleed was in such a critical area of the brain, my doctors decided to try to wait until the swelling subsided a bit before attempting to go in and clip off the ruptured vein.

Misty Watercolor Memories

A few of the memories from my week of waiting and watching:

Even with my life literally hanging in the balance, I'm happy to report my bizarre sense of humor never wavered. I told my brilliant neurosurgeon, Dr. John Hered, "I know this is all in my head." He laughed, despite himself, and told me he'd never had a patient with an attitude quite like mine.

During one of my flatline adventures, I floated above a frantic medical team that was trying to poke thin wires through the skin on my right shoulder and guide them over to the muscles around my heart. They were trying to zap my heart back into beating. I came back inside my body in time to hear one of them caution, "Don't touch her heart!" I KNEW they were going to, though, and they did. I leaped out of my body again into blank oblivion as the monitor attached to my body signaled yet another jump to the other side.

A delightful intern from England was fascinated with my sense of calmness while everyone around me was freaking out, and he and I often spoke when I was conscious. "I must caution you," he said at one point, "that we're giving you some medications to keep you still, and they may cause some hallucinations."

"You mean that little UFO *didn't* just land on my bed?" I asked him in mock distress. He almost fell over laughing.

Another recurring vision during my "week between worlds" was powerful, graphic, and mesmerizing. Now keep in mind, this was in 1989, long before *Lord of the Rings (LOTR)*. But the images I kept tapping into showed me a huge battle being played out between the forces of Darkness, and the forces of Light—a battle that looked for all the world like the horrific scenes depicted in the LOTR trilogy.

There were tanks, and bombs, and infantry, and monsters. There were ghastly faces with rotting flesh, hollow eyes and soulless fury; there were angelic warriors bathed in Light, clad in golden armor and heralded by trumpets, choirs and clouds of eagles. The otherworldly warriors would fly at one another in wave upon wave of attack. Just as suddenly, the visions would vanish, and the "screen" would go completely black. An invisible announcer would say, "We'll be right back, after this…," and I would remember nothing more.

I also don't remember anything about Ed the week I flitted between the worlds of the living and the dead. I *do* remember saying good-by to my older brother who had rushed from his duties as a urologist in Lancaster, Pennsylvania to be by my side. I was so grateful for his calm, loving presence.

It was a truly transcendent time. All my previously held spiritual beliefs, like the interconnectedness of everyone and everything, were proven to me beyond the shadow of a doubt. I could go deeper into a state of Christ Consciousness. I saw the beauty in everything unfolding around me. I also felt the perfect humor in it all. The powerful dream vision I'd been gifted with before the vein in my brain ruptured truly blocked even the tiniest jab of fear. I was in the middle of a spiritual mission, and I had the wheel.

"We're Going In…."

I had the dream June 26th and the aneurysm June 28th. For six days, I flitted in and out of my body, "dying" briefly, then reviving, a number of times. By the 4th of July, even though the brain swelling hadn't significantly diminished, the doctors told me they HAD to operate, or I was just going to STAY dead during one of my little sojourns.

Dr. Hered didn't mince words—it was a serious bleed in the area of my brain that controlled motor skills and language. There was a high probability that I would come out of the operation paralyzed, or mute, or in a complete vegetative state, or not at all. All the odds were against me, except for one fact—I had finally decided to live. I felt I wasn't done yet.

Author Richard Bach, who penned *Jonathan Livingston Seagull*, has a brilliant quote in his book, *Illusions*: "Here is a test to find out if your mission on earth is finished. If you're alive, it's not." I felt no fear, only Divine reassurance that I would come out of everything just fine.

One more funny thing pre-surgery. At the time my head exploded to give me an opportunity to make an early exit if I so desired, I was a TV producer. I had shared with Dr. Hered that one of the popular, sarcastic ways to get someone to chill out was to say, "Hey! Relax! It's only television…it's not brain surgery!" He loved that.

Early the morning of July 4th, as I was lying strapped to the operating room table and the IV had started erasing my consciousness with exquisite finesse, I faintly heard the droning of a razor. One of the nurses began shaving off my curly blond hair. The room was starting to fade away, but suddenly Dr. Hered walked into frame. He bent over the table and gave me a big smile.

"Hey," he grinned. "Relax! It's only brain surgery…it's not television!" I burst into laughter. Then everything went black.

I'm Baaaccckkkkkk….

I have a fuzzy memory of my medical team gathered around my bed in the recovery room, calling my name to get me to come out of the last murky grips of the anesthesia. Everyone was straining to see what my mental clarity was going to be post-surgery. It was a tense moment.

"JONNA!" Dr. Hered was yelling. "CAN YOU HEAR ME? HOW ARE YOU?"

I couldn't disappoint. In a raspy, wispy voice, I murmured, "I have... half a mind... to go back to work."

"She's BACK!" the doctor hooted. Everyone applauded. It was an awesome moment.

I really only remember two things clearly during the next few days in recovery. First of all, I kept refusing morphine as my brain, skull and entire body slowly healed. Instead, I surfed across the top of the pain, observing it, calibrating it, but not being bullied by it.

I gave it a shape, and a color, a size, and a texture. And once I had this image in my mind, I had the power to shrink it down smaller, smaller, smaller—into oblivion. It freaked out members of the medical team, but they knew better than to try to argue with me. Self-hypnosis was NOT a tool they had in their toolbox, but they could see it was definitely working for me.

The other thing was how no one ever offered me a mirror that week. One of my closest friends, then and now, is Elma Broadfoot, former Wichita mayor. Because we knew each other's hearts and minds so well, I couldn't help but notice she was forcing her usual easy smile when she came to visit.

"Elma," I pressed her, "What's wrong?"

"Nothing!" she said, a bit too quickly.

"Elma!" I said again. Suddenly I could feel what she was thinking. "Do you have a mirror?" I asked her.

"You've been through a lot," she said soothingly, patting my arm. She admits now that what she *wanted* to say was, "My GOD, you look like HELL!"

"ELMA! Mirror! Please!" She honestly didn't have one with her, but I was ready at that point to get out of bed and take a few steps. She helped me cross the several feet to the little bathroom. I leaned against the sink for a moment, gripping both sides, with my head bent down. Then I slowly raised my head to meet my gaze in the mirror. The creature that returned my stare was...shocking.

My entire head had swollen to the size of a basketball, with a metal stripe of staples straddling a crimson line that ran from the middle of my head all the way down my scalp, behind my left ear. That glorious curly blond hair with sunny golden highlights was shorn, replaced by random spikes jutting out at irregular angles. My skin and eyes were equally red and swollen.

I continued to stare at my reflection, and the initial revulsion began to dissolve into a grin, then deep laughter. I had found my inner core, where that crazy sense of humor had free reign.

"Are you OK?" Elma asked, rushing in to support me.

"Oh my GOD," I gasped between chuckles. "Elma, I'm Mr. Clean! All I need is a gold hoop earring!" She laughed and hugged me, relieved. She knew I was going to be just fine.

Greener Pastures

As I said before, I believe now that Ed married me so I could care for him in his dotage. The fact that I had just "died," though, punctured *that* balloon for him.

While I was recuperating from my dance with death, he was going on "business trips" to connect with an old girlfriend in the Northwest, who just happened to be a nurse.

I officially found out about the lengthy affair when Ed informed me, in November of the following year, that I had to be out of the house in three weeks. His mistress was coming to spend the holidays with him, and he and I were getting a divorce.

Even though I'd been going through the motions of trying to make the marriage work, I knew on a heart level there just wasn't anything holding us together. Still, Ed's betrayal completely devastated me. It was as if all the stinging hurt and anger of an emotionally tough childhood boiled out of my soul, and flattened me. I remember just collapsing on the kitchen floor sobbing, too broken even to pull myself up on my knees. For this I had decided to live? I cursed the folly of my choice.

As the days melted into weeks, though, I reconnected with my spiritual roots—and regained my strength through prayer and meditation.

I recalled the truths that had given me solace during my adolescence, when I first discovered I wasn't alone in my way of experiencing the world. I stumbled onto an Edgar Cayce book when I was about 12, and eagerly devoured volume after volume about "America's Sleeping Clairvoyant." Reincarnation, psychically picking up impressions about strangers, Atlantis, natural remedies—it was all right there in the books, and it was catnip to me.

Other spiritual lifelines I could cling to included *Life and Teachings of Masters of the Far East, A Course in Miracles, The Seth Material* and Ruth Montgomery, the reporter-turned-Christian Psychic. Her books about psychic Jeanne Dixon, reincarnation, life after death and intuitive abilities nourished and reassured me. Being a young writer myself, I was particularly comforted by Ruth's path from mainstream journalist to psychic practitioner. Maybe I wasn't such a freak after all. The books truly sustained me through a tough adolescence, serving as a special kind of psychic friend and spiritual cheerleader.

Dipping back into these treasured resources of knowledge and guidance helped me remember there was so much more going on than was apparent on the surface. Ed and I were definitely involved in an intense karmic dance. I could be a victim, or I could reclaim my power, heal the imbalances in my life, and get back on my spiritual path. After all, my whole death experience the previous year reminded me I apparently had a big mission this lifetime. Fulfilling one's destiny isn't for wussies! I got my warrior-woman mojo on.

Fighting Fire with Fire

The first thing I did was turn my concern from myself to my colleagues at the television station. Ed was their boss, but I was their friend and confidant. Constantly he would say something curt, confusing, or callus to another employee, and he or she would come downstairs to my office to find out what was going on. Directors, managers, supervisors, crew members—all of them sought my counsel. I was Ed's buffer, interpreter, and caretaker, cleaning up the emotional spills he caused and defusing tense station-wide situations.

Although I would definitely high-tail it out of Wichita the minute I got another job, the Gulf War was underway, and few TV stations or network news departments were hiring. I knew I was going to be stuck still working for Ed for the foreseeable future, and I didn't want the other employees to feel like they were in the middle of another, more local war. It was a small town, and a tight-knit group of people at the station. There was no way our divorce and Ed's affair would remain secret for long. I knew it was up to me to signal that it was okay to acknowledge this shift that would be impossible to ignore.

Mustering up that unflagging sense of humor, I needed the services of a friend at the station, but first I had to confer with him privately about what was about to unfold. The young man was brilliant, passionate, and very upset for me. "None of us ever understood why you married Ed in the first place," he said with unabashed honesty. I had to laugh. He was only too eager to create the project I requested.

The next day, when people arrived for work, they stopped in their tracks when they saw the huge sign on my office door. "IT'S TRUE," the sign read. "WAIT FOR MY BOOK." Most people laughed; obviously relieved they didn't have to pretend they didn't know that Ed and I were divorcing. Some were shocked that I'd come right out and said something. I'm pretty sure that was primarily because I just ruined some truly exciting gossiping opportunities.

The other incident that called on all my warrior woman super powers unfolded at the first department head meeting after I had moved out of the house and into a hotel until I knew what path my life would take. Normally Ed sat at the head of the conference table, and I sat to his right. The engineering director quietly offered me his place several seats away from Ed as we all filed into the room. I squeezed his hand in silent "thank you," but proceeded to my normal chair. I refused to play the wounded victim.

In the course of the meeting, one of the managers mentioned that the 10-second pre-emption announcement for a show change that past weekend hadn't been written and recorded. Those little spots were my responsibility.

"What happened?" Ed roared fiercely, glaring at me. Everyone froze. Most of them knew my old life had pretty much ended over the weekend; some had even helped me gather clothes and personal items and move into the hotel.

I took a deep breath, called on all my spirit guides, and met Ed's hostile gaze that failed to hide his guilt and obvious discomfort at the judgment he knew he was getting from others there. He frequently retreated behind overly dramatic bluster when he was off balance; it helped him maintain the illusion he was still in control.

"Gosh, I just don't know what happened to me this past weekend," I said, shaking my head in mock disgust at my own ineptness. "I just wasn't myself to let that announcement slip. I am SO sorry. It won't happen again."

The simultaneous sharp intake of breath on the part of the rest of the meeting-goers was clearly audible. Their heads shifted from looking at me to looking at Ed as if they were watching a cerebral tennis tournament. He dropped his eyes to the table and his doughy features flushed bright red.

Game! Set! Match! My win!

On the way out of the room at the close of the meeting, just about everyone either touched me or smiled their encouragement. It was going to be difficult being there for a while, but I was going to make it.

Even though it was a tough transition, this emotionally devastating divorce was the bridge to what was about to become the happiest time of my life. But first, I took a break from the drama in Wichita to fly back East for Christmas with my family in Pennsylvania. As I was spiritually purging from half a decade with Ed, I knew I had to exorcise a few more ghosts from my childhood that helped facilitate that bad marriage in the first place.

Chapter 3
Welcome to Earth!

I used my time on the flight from Kansas to Pennsylvania for a bit of a life review. Newly single and still smarting from the betrayal I had refused to acknowledge consciously as it unfolded, I knew I could no longer try to repress my considerable intuitive ability in a relationship, or a job. If I couldn't openly express my spiritual truths with a man, he definitely wasn't the man for me. Sure, it might mean I would be walking a lonely path—but honestly, is there anything more lonely than being in a marriage where you feel you have absolutely no real connection to your spouse? As a born psychic, I'd already been walking a rather solitary road as long as I could remember.

Most kids have that inevitable split from their parents— that moment when they first realize the people who spawned them *aren't* unquestionably accurate, limitless founts of vast stores of wisdom—when they're in their teens.

I was four.

Mom put me to bed in the family's circa-1750s Pennsylvania farmhouse that Dad had been remodeling since we'd moved in years before. My turquoise teddy bear-studded Dr. Denton's swaddled my little frame in flannel, and my platinum tresses splayed across the pillow as Mom kissed me goodnight. "Sleep tight, sweetie," she called to me as she descended the creaking, winding stairs leading back down to the first floor.

Just as I was starting to drift off to the soft strains of classical music emanating from the old gray radio in the hallway, I began to feel strange. Instead of the sweet, dark nothingness that usually wrapped me in slumber, I was aware of an odd pulling sensation in my chest. Suddenly I was floating above my motionless body, looking down at it. I slowly began drifting towards the staircase, puzzled but simultaneously delighted at this nocturnal "air surfing."

Drawn by the sound of my parents' conversation, I was soon hovering near the kitchen ceiling, looking down on my mom and dad. They were sitting at the table, talking earnestly, sipping coffee from orange Melmac cups.

"MOM!" I hollered, flailing my arms to get her attention. "DAD! I'm up HERE!" They continued their discussion, oblivious to the fact I was a few feet overhead. "I'm *right here!*" I hollered again. Nothing.

I was more frustrated at their lack of response than frightened because I was flying. I eventually floated back upstairs and dropped into my body with a jerk. Immediately I hopped out of bed and dashed back down those narrow winding stairs.

"I JUST FLEW DOWN HERE," I exclaimed, "AND YOU DIDN'T SEE ME! YOU DIDN'T HEAR ME! I WAS FLOATING RIGHT *THERE*!" I insisted, jabbing the space above the table with my little forefinger.

"Well goodness sakes!" Dad said with exaggerated enthusiasm. "What a great little imagination you have!"

"It really *happened*!" I insisted, exasperated. "I *really* flew down here!"

"You are such a creative storyteller, dear," Mom said soothingly. "Now go back to bed, honey. It's late."

I remember standing there in those little Dr. Denton's, incredulous that they were unconvinced. I had just *experienced* it. I *knew* it was real! Dejected, I drooped my head, and slowly trudged back upstairs.

"Goodnight, dear," Mom called after me.

At this point, please let me interject that this entire experience is *nothing* out of the ordinary for nearly every child. *Everyone* is psychic, and has natural intuitive ability. Particularly when they're kids, and their minds are wide open to discovery and learning, people can have spectacular experiences that they're SO eager to share.

Because our society traditionally prefers to suppress and ignore extra-sensory phenomena, kids quickly get the message it's not okay, or valid, or even appropriate to experience *or* discuss any of this stuff. "Quit daydreaming," we're told. "Don't color that tree purple! Trees are supposed to be green!" "Nancy is an imaginary friend—stop making up stuff about her!" "Grandma's dead—she CAN'T be sitting on the couch!" "Of COURSE you don't know what the dog is thinking! That's just silly!"

In my family, particularly, anything I said or did that fell outside the narrow confines of "normalcy" resulted in my being taunted, ignored, punished or forced to recant the stories I knew in my heart to be true.

Dad was a machine shop teacher in the Allentown School District, and my parents constantly demanded that my two brothers—one three years older than me, one four years younger—and I, remain beyond reproach in our tight-knit city. We were instructed constantly to be model students and children, staying below the radar and out of trouble because, according to Mom, we were closely scrutinized by apparently everyone. Having a little psychic in the family was simply out of the question. My father would hum the *Twilight Zone* music when I tried to talk about my experiences, and he cut short any possible discussion about the things I knew to be real.

When children hear their experiences being lampooned enough times, they soon learn it's much easier, and less hurtful, simply to pretend nothing is happening. They begin to shut down their natural intuitive ability, and seal the door to a whole glorious dimension of their existence—a door that will remain closed unless they decide to study quantum physics; read 1 Corinthians 12–14 in which the Apostle Paul details all the spiritual gifts people receive, including intuitive ability; or pay a heck of a lot of money to relearn how to relax, meditate and be creative.

The reason I didn't just shut it down, even though Mom and Dad discounted my "night flight," was because of something else wonderful that happened that evening. In my dreams, I found myself perched on one end of the old-fashioned clothesline that stood sentry in the back yard, just beyond the foundation of the house's 200-year-old outdoor brick oven. Although I couldn't *see* anyone, I very clearly heard gentle voices saying, "We know you can do it! Come on now!" Slowly, tentatively, I flew to the other side of the clothesline, using the parallel ropes below me as a guide.

"Well done!" those encouraging voices congratulated me as I landed, pajama clad feet first, on the metal cross bar. "Now, turn around and come on back!"

Every night those invisible "friends," who I now know were spirit guides and guardian angels, would teach me how to navigate in the astral world. I learned how to fly, or astral project; how to see colors and energies around people, places and things; how to zone in on what people were thinking, and even how to gaze into a person's eyes, breathe deeply, and see his or her current physical manifestation fade away, and another one come into focus. This new image showed me who he or she had been in another place and time, and the forms weren't always human. They weren't always attractive or nice, either.

Because I kept getting this regular reinforcement and instruction, I was able to endure my dad ridiculing me when I spoke about what I was experiencing. Eventually, I just pretty much stopped talking about all the fascinating things happening in my little corner of the world, but I didn't shut them down. I bristled when my parents—or any grownups—dismissed my questions about ghosts, ESP, UFOs, talking to animals or Jesus, or when what I talked about was simply labeled "a child's wild imagination." I felt hurt, and like an outsider, because of the relentless teasing, but I also knew these things were real. I was living them

The Brown Violin

When I was about eight, a little friend of mine started taking violin lessons. We were creating new wardrobes for our Barbie dolls at her house one day when I saw her violin sitting on a chair in the family room. I felt drawn to it, so I walked over, picked it up, and started playing. I mean PLAYING, not just making noise. Her dad, a school psychologist who was also in the room, immediately leaped to his feet.

"How long have you been taking lessons?" he demanded.

I froze in mid-bow and stared back at him.

"HOW LONG?" he barked again. My friend was also staring at me, gape-mouthed. I was terrified at their reactions, and remember putting the little instrument down, never to pick up a violin again. I was so freaked by their shock that I have never even learned to read music.

I wonder how many other little musicians shut down their gifts when their intuitive talent defies a logical progression of years of study and practice first, *then* some degree of musical proficiency. It was also pretty much the turning point for that friendship. Because her father was so undone by my instant ability to play the violin, my playmate also started to keep her distance.

I learned early that people fear things they can't understand. That little drama, I realized in retrospect, was starting to teach me the importance of using humor to defuse a tense situation when my psychic gifts freaked people out. I have since realized that had I been able to make the two of them laugh instead of back away, it could have been a completely different outcome.

Ghostly Cool

Another childhood memory floated into my mind as I watched the flat plains of the Midwest segue into the wrinkled terrain of the Appalachians from my window seat on the plane.

Summers in Pennsylvania are stifling hot, particularly in 200-year old homes with no air conditioning. Even the setting of the sun doesn't offer any real relief from the sticky, humid air that's thick enough to choke a toad. (I've watched waaayyy too many Dan Rather newscasts.)

It was on just such a night when I was about eight that I awoke from a deep sleep to see a glowing woman, transparent and garbed in colonial dress, standing by my bedside, watching me. I screamed. In seconds, my parents charged through the door and flicked on the overhead light.

"WHAT'S WRONG?" Mom yelled.

"THERE WAS A GHOST!" I answered

"It was just a dream," my father said, obviously relieved it wasn't a *real* alarm. I wanted to protest that the image was VERY real, but sadly realized it would be a futile argument, and would definitely end in ridicule and maybe my tears. I stayed silent.

"Good night, dear," my mom said as they retreated out the door. Then, Dad stopped, and looked around my room one more time.

"It sure is cold in here," he said with curiosity. Then he shrugged and followed Mom back to their room.

I wouldn't know the particulars until years later, but in metaphysical circles, it's well known that disembodied entities will change thermal energy into electromagnetic energy to manifest. This will create a cold spot like the one in my room that steamy summer night.

It's also important to note that my visitor wasn't threatening me at all—she was actually quite kind. She just startled me.

Instead of being able to share that with my parents, or talk about how the whole event made me feel, I swallowed my emotions completely. The relentless teasing from my father would have been too painful. My reluctance that night to be completely honest about what was happening with me psychically was definitely setting a pattern that would repeat throughout much of my life. As the airplane flight took me further from Ed, it brought me closer to understanding how my early experiences made me vulnerable to Ed's advances in the first place.

"Follow the thread," spiritual teachers tell us. "See how it leads you back to your childhood." Anything that inspires an emotional reaction has a life beyond what appears to be happening in the moment. It's part of a thread woven into the rich tapestry of your past. When was the last time you felt this? And then, the tougher question—when was the *first* time? Discover that trigger by following that thread, and you can heal the hurt.

Loose Threads

The flight attendants came down the aisles of the plane, offering little prepackaged meal trays. I welcomed the brief incursion into my somber introspective journey, and politely refused the calorie-dense snack. It reminded me that Ed was always making critical comments about my weight. Ohhhh—another thread....

My father's parents split up when he was a baby, long before divorce claimed half of all marriages. He grew up a pawn his mother sacrificed mercilessly in her on-going battle to hurt his dad, who was 18 years her senior. From the vantage point of several decades, I could understand Dad never had any concept of what constituted a loving family dynamic. He couldn't break the cycle of sarcasm and coldness because he didn't know what the alternatives could be.

He delighted in ridiculing my intuitive abilities, and laughingly referred to me frequently as his "big, husky daughter." That esteem-squashing moniker was spawned one weekend when I was helping Dad develop pictures in the darkroom at the middle school where he taught machine shop.

One of the janitors stopped by to say hello, and Dad told the man how I helped him carry sheetrock up the home's winding stairs in Dad's on-going efforts to "finish the house." It was built in the 1750s, and he planned to do the remodeling himself. Despite his best intentions, the house had a two-century head start, and defied his efforts to update it. I always believed the Occupational Safety and Health Administration (OSHA) would have condemned the dilapidated structure with its concave floors balancing atop rotting support beams precariously braced against the dirt floor of the home's coal cellar. The kitchen was temporarily in the living room for four decades.

The janitor was a tall, rough, doughy man with a vacant look and retreating hairline. "It's so great you have a big, husky daughter who can carry sheetrock!" he said, gesturing towards me. As Dad's laughter mingled with the janitor's, a little piece of me died. That very moment, my weight became the barometer of my happiness, and a frequent source of pain and embarrassment. Like Dad, Ed had found that tender spot, and pounced on it. Look at any of my pictures, and you'll be able to calibrate my level of pain at any particular age by what I'm weighing at the time.

This high-altitude life review was excruciating, but illuminating. My thoughts drifted to Mom's influence in my life.

Sparking Excitement

Basic science teaches us that we are comprised of energy in motion, with protons and electrons zipping around the nucleus of every atom in each of our 100 trillion cells. All of this results in quite an impressive electrical field, or aura, around each of us.

Some people easily can detect this colorful cocoon of energy surrounding us; others can learn to sense or see this very individualized light show. I was one of those kids who just always saw the energy around people and things, and just assumed everyone else did, too.

I always saw that the color, size, density, and shape of this aura everyone had changed constantly, depending on their energy level, emotions, and physical health.

I specifically remember tormenting my mother when I was about 11 just to make her angry, and watch the orange sparks fly off of her. I do NOT recommend this to other kids!

Mom might even have suspected what I was doing. She herself is deeply intuitive, and has chosen to repress her considerable gifts. I recall two notable exceptions. First, when she was four, she insisted she be driven to the farm where her father was working so she could hug him. It was a joyful, affectionate encounter, and the last time she saw him alive. He died later that day from appendicitis.

For the other, I was white-water rafting with friends in the Nantahala River in Tennessee when I was 27, and was tossed overboard when we hit some Class 4 rapids. I slammed my head on a rock and despite my helmet, was knocked unconscious. I survived because a quick-thinking friend latched on to my life jacket and held my head above water until they could get the raft—and me—to the riverbank. I didn't want to worry my family back in Pennsylvania, so I didn't call to tell them about it. Instead, Mom called me, frantic, demanding to know that I was okay. Bottom line, she didn't want to talk about her own psychic ability. And she definitely didn't want me to openly use mine. Even if things came to me in dreams....

"Someone's Looking for You!"

My dreams were never just "dreams"—they were always full-color, surround sound adventures packed with information, warnings, flying, maps, music, tastes, aromas, fascinating people I'm about to meet and interesting things I'm about to encounter. I've learned to pay attention and honor my dreams.

Following this thread led me back to a very vivid dream I had one night when I was a kid. In it, a beautiful cat with feathers sprouting from her neck appeared and gazed at me through her spectacular glowing amber eyes. She was magnificent, with golden, chocolate, ebony, and white hairs woven together in a vibrant tapestry of color.

"Hello, Jonna," she said in a sweet, low voice. "My name is Tapestry, and I've been looking for you." In my dream, I reached out to pet her, but I was awakened by my dad calling up the stairs for me to get up.

"There's someone down here looking for you," he called. Groggily I crawled out of bed and came down the winding staircase.

"Out here," he said. I walked through the kitchen and out onto the back porch to see—Tapestry! She just sat there, waiting for me, then walked up to me and let me pet her. The "neck feathers" I'd seen in the dream were really a full ruff, and the warm colors of her fur blended perfectly into that same rich fabric. She had, indeed, been looking for me.

One of the funniest things I remember about this powerful feline companion was Mom frequently screaming for me to come get her. The washer and dryer were down in the coal cellar, and after Mom would head down the stairs with a load of clothes, Tapestry would take up her perch halfway down the stairs and sit there, perfectly still, just staring at Mom. My poor mother was terrified by Tapestry's otherworldly presence, and always hollered for me to come get her so she could get back up the stairs and into the house.

Cone of Silence

The loud grating of metal on metal jolted me back to the present. The plane's landing gear was coming down, the wing flaps were going up, and I made the decision to keep my psychic transmissions safely stowed away for the duration of this visit. I was already feeling emotional as I worked to heal both a shattered heart and wounded ego. It seemed pointless to make myself vulnerable to sarcastic digs about the "vibes" I was getting. My shields were up.

Meanwhile, on the psychic level, I was still unaware that out in sunny Southern California, Mickey Mouse and the love of my life were waiting for me. First, though, there were a few more threads demanding my immediate attention.

Chapter 4
Going Underground

After surviving our turbulent, rambunctious childhood without killing one another, my brothers and I had become quite close. Jeff and I frequently went back and forth about psychic phenomena; he came from a more biblical perspective, and we challenged and stretched each other's minds through the decades while having fascinating and inspiring conversations. Dave, meanwhile, wasn't into the metaphysical field at all, but was very warm, loving, and generous with his time and his caring. I loved them both dearly, and it was wonderful feeling their support. Both brothers were married to wonderful women, and ironically, each had four kids—three daughters, with the youngest being a son. The combined families were eager to include me in their Christmas festivities.

In my family, we've always shown "love" with food, so Mom tried to make every single dish I ever liked. Even Dad was less intense than usual. No one in the family had really liked Ed, but they all tried to be polite while we were married. Now, the gloves were off.

Though I appreciated their enthusiasm in renaming him "Loather, Lord of the Underworld," I found myself content just to allow both the physical and emotional distance between Ed and Allentown shift my precarious emotional state. I was still unraveling threads, determined to heal my sensitive heart by getting to the root of why I had settled for someone who was so unsuited for me.

My parents insisted on doing one of the little holiday rituals from childhood—driving around to find the prettiest Christmas lights. I agreed. It meant we wouldn't be sitting in a living room, staring at one another. It would not be obvious to anyone when I projected out of my body as my thoughts took me far, far away, from what was happening inside that old Chevy station wagon during our ride.

Healing Memories

One twinkling street faded into the next; then I recognized the church where I had covered the lecture of psychic Helen Schreiber nearly 20 years earlier. My mind jumped back to the night Helen not only told me I was here to raise world consciousness, but also that I was a healer. I remembered after her lecture that night, I approached Helen to find out more about how to harness my supposed healing ability.

"Come to a healing session and watch the practitioners," she had suggested.

A few nights later, I arrived at Helen's home to observe other healers in action. It was quite simple—each healer would stand behind a person who was seated in a chair, raise his or her left hand with the fingers pointed upwards and the palm exposed, and put the right hand about three inches over the top of the seated person's head.

"They're drawing energy in from the universe with their left hand," Helen explained, "and with their right hand, they're feeling the energy around the person's crown chakra."

Note: Dr. Candace Pert is a brilliant scientist who, she jokes in her own words, "became mystical in my old age." She's proven the ancient metaphysical teaching that the body doesn't have just one brain, but rather seven major energy centers going up the spinal column, each with a specific consciousness and influencing a key aspect of our lives. The one on the top of the head, the crown chakra, connects people into Christ Consciousness, or the Universal Field, as quantum physicists call it.

Helen invited me to try it. Immediately as I raised my left hand, I felt waves of invisible energy washing over me, and my right hand became very hot. Chills raced up my spine.

"Wow," the person seated in the chair in front of me exclaimed. "I feel that already!" It was blissful to be able to try out this new facet of my gifts, and to get instant feedback that I could actually make a positive difference with the abilities I'd previously struggled to conceal. That very evening I learned that unleashing healing energy is as simple as desiring to do so. Everyone is a healer. Anyone can choose to channel that gift merely by willing it so. "Ask, and it is given…."

"Look!" Mom said cheerfully, bringing me back to the present, and the "prettiest light display" quest. "These houses got together to do the 12 Days of Christmas!"

"Groovy!" I said, lapsing into the annoying language I used when I was a teen.

"And there's Allen—your old high school. Remember Mrs. Bixler?"

Mrs. B, the journalism teacher, was about the *only* positive thing I remembered from those three years. She totally got me—my bizarre sense of humor, my passion to write, and even my uncanny intuition. Gazing at the imposing front entrance columns through the frost-kissed car window stirred up a quagmire of old memories better left unearthed.

While I loved learning how to channel my psychic healing abilities through Helen's classes, I stayed pretty guarded in high school. I was in the popular group, co-editing the school paper and singing in the choir, even joining the Color Guard for a year so I could go to band camp. But I still had to tread carefully about revealing too much psychic stuff, and I felt everything on a painfully deep level. I frequently felt like I was "hiding in plain sight." That's why being able to learn how to heal, and continuing to read all the spiritual material I could get my hands on, was so important to me. It helped me find a kind of balance, even though I still rarely let my friends know about all the information I was constantly receiving and processing.

My increasing sensitivity made me much more open to what people were thinking and feeling. I remember really wanting to take the psychology class my senior year, but having a sick, queasy feeling about the teacher. I convinced him to let me do an independent study project comparing and contrasting Edgar Cayce and Sigmund Freud. I think he gave me an "A" because he was somewhat frightened of me. But gently refocusing.... this teacher was eventually arrested—twice!—for taking indecent liberties with a minor. I had picked up that aspect of his character even though I couldn't specifically say *why* I felt ill around him at the time.

"Do you want to call any of your old college friends?" Mom asked, reeling me back into the present moment, and our Lightsapalooza tour.

"Ummmm...probably not this trip," I answered. Probably not EVER, I said silently. Her question triggered a new flood of memories I'd mentally covered with several feet of cement decades ago.

The Ring (NO, Not That Movie!)

In college, I really began experimenting with my growing abilities. I didn't yet have a good spiritual base for what I was doing, so God only knows what type of energy I might have been tapping into as I "played" in other dimensions. In retrospect, I know my guardian angels have shoulder pads, shin guards, strong helmets and a LOT of patience, because I never got into any serious trouble with the Dark Side. I also know this is precisely why I have a custom license plate that reads, "PRAY," and why I constantly teach people to put themselves in protective Divine White Light. Did you read the affirmation at the front of the book? It's the one I have printed on cards, and that I hand out to everyone who will take one.

"Being psychic" should never be the goal. When we make our spiritual development the priority goal, and make our link to "God"—however we conceive of that idea—the strongest connection we have, then psychic abilities just naturally begin to manifest. NOW I understand that concept, and teach it.

Nevertheless, back in college, it was all just flying by the seat of my pants, and putting on a great show. All I knew was: this was FUN. At last I didn't have to hide what I could do as I did when I lived at home, and I jumped in with both feet.

During midterms my sophomore year, I remember thinking at one of the Communications professors, "What's the answer to number 4?" Just as suddenly, I "knew" the right answer. I got a perfect score, and frequently made Dean's List.

I levitated those heavy wooden spool tables at frat parties; made pendulums out of rings and thread to answer accurately questions for students I'd never met, and held séances in the dorm, while mobiles hanging from the ceiling jerked back and forth and caps exploded off of soda bottles. I would also transfigure into an Indian during the circles which completely freaked out all my dorm mates.

One day a girl on my dorm floor got up the courage to approach me. "If you're so good at weird stuff," she challenged, "Can you find my ring that I lost yesterday?"

"OK," I said, "Come with me." I led her outside, and told her just to start walking; I would walk beside her. It was a huge campus, with intersecting webs of sidewalks, large grassy expanses and dozens of buildings. As word spread about what was happening, more and more people started trailing after us, giggling, whispering and nudging one another.

After about 15 minutes of walking next to her in silence, I stopped. She, and the throng behind us, also halted. I reached down into the grass, picked up her silver ring, and handed it to her. The girl stared at the ring, dumbfounded. Then, with the rest of the crowd, she turned and dashed back to the dorm, screaming. I knew from past experience the best way to defuse the rather tense situation was simply to act as if nothing out of the norm had just happened. Because I didn't make a big deal of out it, neither did anyone else. My growing psychic abilities became the elephant in the living room about which no one really talked.

Driven to Excel

Since my classmates viewed me with a mixture of varying degrees of fear and awe, I was very driven to establish strong credibility by real world standards. I didn't try to hide my psychic abilities in college, but at the same time, I focused on excelling in class and extra curricular activities. I ended up being the first freshman feature writer for the college paper before being named assistant editor, then editor. I converted the paper from the old Linotype system to cold type, and even designed and built the light tables to do the layout. I also became the yearbook photographer.

Even people who thought I was strange came to me for mini-psychic readings to help them with relationships, health issues, or concerns about classes. When I mentioned to a classmate that I was going to do a séance in the basement of the chapel, word spread across campus like wildfire. As I started heading toward the building that evening, I saw literally hundreds of students gathering, waiting for me. Many of them were stoned or drunk.

When I saw the freak-fest that was waiting for me outside the chapel, I just turned around and went back to my dorm. I never tried that again!

A quick word about mind-altering substances—I don't like them, trust them, or use them.

Earlier I mentioned how we each have seven chakras, or major energy centers in the body. Through prayer, meditation, and study we can gently dissolve the veils covering each and access the energies and abilities the chakras gift to us. When they are activated respectfully and intentionally, we can direct the resulting energies in a positive, effective, and safe way.

On the other hand, using drugs or alcohol pierces the veils in a potentially negative and dangerous fashion, twisting and mutating the energies in ways that are frequently dark, unpleasant, and threatening on physical, mental, emotional, and spiritual levels. I can see demonic or reptilian features on people who are tripping or drunk, and avoid being around that lower energy.

Independent Study

At what was then called Rider College, we had the option of taking the month of January off to tour Europe if our parents had the money, or doing a three-credit "Independent Study Project" if our parents did not. This required creating a proposal, getting the approval of a faculty sponsor, and then doing a report at the end of the study outlining the results.

Because I was flexing my metaphysical muscles, I convinced one of my professors to sponsor a "Natural Healing" project. The structure of the study was simple— either he or I would find sick students, bring them up to his office, and then, while he timed me with his stopwatch, I'd heal them.

By that point fellow students pretty much knew what I did, and were eager to participate. People with headaches, bruises, fevers—even a cheerleader with a pulled hamstring— lined up for relief.

I would seat them, then stand beside them with my left hand up to pull in Universal energy, and my right hand a few inches from the top of their heads to direct the energy into them. As soon as I felt the warmth and electricity indicating we had a connection, I would be drawn to the parts of their bodies that were in pain. I never touched them; rather, I worked in their energy fields.

While I focused on getting the students back in alignment, my professor stood there observing, with the tick-tick-tick of his stopwatch filling the silence in the room.

One by one, they'd come in hurting, and walk out smiling. My poor advisor couldn't really explain what the heck was going on, but he was a good sport about just documenting it.

That study still might exist somewhere in the school's files.

An Excellent Pupil

The same dorm mate who lost her ring also had a congenital eye defect, a weak muscle in one eye, and couldn't follow moving objects with both eyes simultaneously. Several intensive surgeries hadn't corrected the problem.

After she heard about the healing project, she asked me if I could heal her eye.

"Well, let's give it a try," I answered.

While she perched on a chair in her dorm room, I stood behind her, with my hands a few inches from her body. Her roommate watched us quizzically.

As I calibrated the consistency of the blockages she had, I could feel surges of both hot and cold energy while my hands moved from the top of her head around to her face. I pulled strands of cloudy energy from the space just inches in front of her eyes and flicked my hands to cast it off. For several minutes I continued working in her energy field, never physically touching her.

When I felt the energy had shifted, I flicked my hands again to release anything I had pulled from her, and reached for a pencil on her desk. I held the pencil about two feet in front of her face.

"I'm going to bring this pencil close to your nose," I told her, "and I want you to follow it with both your eyes."

Her roommate and I watched her carefully as I slowly moved the pencil closer, closer, closer to her face. Both of her eyes tracked it perfectly. I smiled and stood up.

"I think you're good now," I said. Both she and her roommate were staring at me, gape-mouthed. "Gotta go!" I said, and hastily retreated out the door. From that point on, as far as I know, the woman never had any additional problems with her eye coordination. We never mentioned anything about the session, which was just fine with me. My pattern of not making a big deal about what I did, or making a quick joke about it, pretty much kept everyone else from overreacting, too. I was just happy to be able to use my ability to help people after keeping it hidden away for so many years.

Pirate Recall

One dramatic incident during my sophomore year showed me the power of our natural intuitive ability, even if we don't necessarily believe in it. I was dating a senior who was an economics and accounting double major, a far cry from my normal "comfort zone" of creativity, writing, and intuitive phenomena.

This particular day, we were in "Rick's" room talking. I was sitting on his bed while he was sitting on a chair. I don't even remember what we were talking about, but I DO remember classical music coming on the radio. Suddenly, I was paralyzed. As I stared at Rick, he became a pirate, standing on his ship, staring over the railing in horror. I felt as though everything was happening in slow motion, and I was aware that he was staring into the water at me. I was dead, and starting to sink to the bottom of the sea. I couldn't move, I couldn't scream, I couldn't understand what the heck was happening to me.

Meanwhile, in real life, Rick, too, had become paralyzed on the chair, and was literally staring at me in horror. He fell off the chair and crashed onto the floor. It seemed like hours, but it was actually only seconds before we could both move and speak again.

"WHAT JUST HAPPENED?" he yelled at me.

"WHAT DID YOU SEE?" I screamed back at him.

Gradually we calmed down and were able to exchange details.

"You were dead, in the water...." Rick began explaining. "I didn't know you were on that ship when we fired at it."

"OhmyGOD, we were in the same place!" I said. "You were a PIRATE!"

As we pieced together the strange experience, we realized we had both just participated in some kind of a powerful shared "past life" memory. In a flash, I saw the whole back-story. I was the daughter of an aristocratic English family, and I had fallen in love with the pirate. My parents were aghast, and were shipping me off to another part of the country to separate us permanently.

Rick the pirate, not knowing I was on that ship, attacked it. I was killed, and knocked overboard. He was horrified when he recognized my body floating on the ocean's surface. After we shared our perspective of the bizarre time warp, we just stared at each other. How could we have "imagined" the exact same incident—and what was that wave of energy that literally knocked Rick to the floor and pinned me down so tightly I couldn't move for several seconds?

Neither one of us really could explain effectively what had happened. Even though we gamely attempted to continue our friendship, that particular "adventure" was just too weird to be able to ignore. We just ended up drifting apart, like two ships passing in the night.

"No, I don't think I'll try to get in touch with any of the people I knew in college," I said again, as our Christmas lights tour of Allentown drew to a close. "I'm not feeling very social right now." And, they're probably all still scared stiff of me, I thought. Decades later, they're probably still talking about how the caps shot off the soda bottles, how I transfigured into an Indian, or how they fell off a chair and had a morbid vision of me, dead.

I vowed to just turn my brain off for the rest of the evening and watch the Rudolph animated Christmas special. I'd done enough time-travel and thread-following for the moment. I knew the morning would bring some bigger ghosts with which to deal.

Chapter 5
It's Harder to Ignore It

The next morning at breakfast, I opened the newspaper and was immediately dragged back down memory lane. For my first few years right out of college, the reporters and editors who created the daily reality for the folks in the Lehigh Valley with that very newspaper were my colleagues, bosses, and friends. It was a time of great discovery and really starting to understand the magnitude of the psychic ability I had. Thrilled with my shift from college student to cub reporter, I moved into my own apartment and was talking openly about metaphysics with anyone who would listen. To my delight, many fellow reporters did. I started doing regular readings for friends, and it became a pretty normal routine for all of us.

One particular evening a fellow reporter, Sandi Matuschka, called in a panic. The guy she was going out with hadn't shown up for their dinner date, and she was concerned. I immediately "went to level," and received a vivid, appalling image. When I dissolved it, it sprang back into my consciousness with crystal clear detail.

"Sandi," I told her slowly, "I'm so sorry! I see the body of your friend in the cab of a green truck. He's been shot, and he's dead. The truck is at a construction site, somewhere they're building a bridge."

She and I were in tears, and frantically tried to figure out if we should call the police. Since we were both reporters and had a certain amount of credibility we needed to maintain, we hesitated to report a "murder" vision, and decided to wait.

The next day the guy showed up. He'd been out drinking with buddies, and completely spaced his date with Sandi. I was glad he was alive, but I was horrified I had received such an incorrect image, and such a grisly one at that.

Three years later both Sandi and I were in different jobs, and I was in a different state—she was a system editor with the Morning Call, and I was a TV producer in Miami. I was surprised to get a call from her out of the blue.

"I just thought you should know," she said. "They've found the body of my friend, in the cab of a green truck. He'd been shot dead at a construction site, where they were building a bridge."

Every detail I had seen in my vision was exactly correct—I was just three years early. To me this is another proof of what physicists teach—that everything is happening simultaneously, and through rips, folds, or wormholes in the fabric of time and space, we can experience these overlaps or precognitive flashes.

Astara Adventure

Back to my memories from that heavy Christmas visit of finding the triggers and following those threads....

Another way I nourished my psychic side while reporting for the newspaper was reading every spiritual book I could get my hands on. I also discovered Astara. This ancient mystery school was founded by Robert and Earlyne Chaney, and they hosted conferences around the country, spoke, led healing sessions, and created books like the one Earlyne did with the Moosewood Cookbook folks.

Sandi, the same reporter friend from the Green Truck Incident, was also interested in studying the spiritual dimensions of life, and learned Earlyne was hosting an Astara weekend conference in Ft. Lauderdale. I jumped at her invitation to go along.

I was only 21 at the time, and I'd never been on a plane. We arrived early at the Philadelphia airport, and had dinner there before our flight. Feeling adventurous, I ordered the turtle soup, which arrived with a small carafe of sherry.

Being a naive kid from a small town, I had never eaten turtle soup, and didn't realize the appropriate thing to do was simply splash a bit of the sherry into my bowl. Instead, I emptied the entire carafe as the waiter gasped. Do I even need to tell you I don't remember a heck of a lot about getting on the plane, and the first few hours of the flight? Awesome soup, though!

I DID sober up by the time we landed, and was *so* excited about the possibility of meeting Earlyne. As we checked into our hotel, Sandi and I were thrilled to learn Earlyne was inviting conference participants to an informal "meet and greet" session in one of the hotel banquet rooms. We dashed to our room, dumped our suitcases, did a quick hair-and-makeup fix, and headed back downstairs to find the Astara group.

A line of people of all ages snaked outside the conference room door, and we could see Earlyne herself, garbed in a long, flowing white robe, standing just inside the doorway, greeting guests. I could feel my heart racing with excitement.

Sandi was in front of me, and as she entered the door Earlyne shook her hand, smiled, and thanked her for coming. Then she turned to me, and took both my hands in hers.

"I've been waiting for you, dear," she said warmly. "Will you help me with the healing session tomorrow night?"

My jaw dropped to the floor, but I managed to nod "Yes." Sandi guided me into the banquet room, but the rest of that evening, and even Earlyne's workshops the next day, remained a blur to me. I was excited, frightened, honored, and overwhelmed. What could I possibly contribute to Earlyne's session? And even worse, what if I tried to help, and nothing happened? A thousand fears and questions tumbled through my mind. I finally realized I could make myself nuts by continuing to dwell on what might go wrong, or else I could just do the little affirmation, and turn it all over to God. Despite my emotional turmoil, I still trusted that anything I did in His name would be the right thing.

The conference schedule called for a group dinner, then we were to reconvene in the hotel auditorium later that evening for the final event—Earlyne's healing session.

This happened decades ago, but I remember this part clear as day. Earlyne stood at the front of the room and spoke into a microphone, inviting people to be healed. I stood to the side, facing the audience, silently praying for divine guidance. Six burly guys, three on each side of me, waited for conference participants to come stand in front of me. I put my right hand on their foreheads, and they'd drop like flies. That's where those six burly guys came in—they caught them and gently lowered them to the floor.

Then I'd put my hands on their heads, or stomachs, or legs, or wherever I just "felt" something was wrong with them, and I would feel things moving inside of them. I don't mean like a simple heartbeat, or their chests rising and falling with a deep breath. I mean like things LURCHING up, down, around—the only thing I can possibly compare it to is what it would feel like to have your hands in the water when a dense throng of hungry fish are competing for food pellets.

I would "know" when to finish, and the people were crying and praising God, and generally quite happy with whatever it was I had just done. I'm making no claims blind people suddenly saw or lame people leaped out of wheelchairs. What I am saying is that SOMETHING amazing was going on, and people were transforming. I have no idea how long we continued to work with folks—it was as though I were on autopilot. I just turned it all over to The Reliable Source.

After the last person who desired a treatment had been served, the conference concluded, and we went back to our rooms. Sandi and I ended up going out to the hotel pool and flopping into chaise lounges to stare up at the starry night sky. I was too blown away by what had just happened even to try to put words to it.

Instead, I sat back, closed my eyes, and continued to feel hot, powerful energy surging up my spinal column and erupting out the top of my head. Time and space stopped for me, and my tears started to flow freely. I don't know how long I sobbed—there was just no way to stop this release of energy and emotions so deep and so strong, coming from a place in my soul I didn't even know I had. It was my first full Kundalini rising experience. My tears were a cleansing and heart-felt expression of gratitude to be in that place, at that time, for those people.

When I finally stopped crying and opened my eyes, the sky had changed. Oh, all the stars were still there, reflecting in the hotel pool. But for the first time ever, I saw a spectacular neon violet grid that appeared to curve right around the earth. It was as if the planet were surrounded by a humongous energetic "net," which glowed brilliantly in the ink black sky. I immediately realized I was seeing what would now be called "Intergalactic GPS." Every spot on the earth could quickly be accessed from space with the correct positioning information—and that could be determined with this heavenly grid. Of course! It made so much sense. I know other people have actually seen this spectacular celestial light show because the grid I first encountered that night is used in the current scientific depiction of wormholes. SOMEONE's got it right!

No Dessert, Thank You

Shortly after Sandi and I returned to our work at the newspaper, I was still processing all the events of that transformational weekend in Ft. Lauderdale. I shared what had happened in the healing session with a guy I was dating casually.

"Wow, that's really something!" he said. The next day, he told me his aunt wanted to have us come to dinner at her place, and we picked an evening.

The gathering started out pleasantly enough. We chit-chatted about the weather and some articles I'd recently written as we passed around the fried chicken, green beans and mashed potatoes. His aunt and uncle seemed a bit intense, but I just attributed that to my being a little nervous at meeting "family" this early in our relationship.

Then, the wind shifted.

"Tell them about your Florida weekend," my date urged.

Pleased to oblige, I had just gotten to the part about putting my hand on a person's forehead and watching them fall, when both the aunt and uncle leaped up from their chairs, and ran to either side of me. They pressed their hands on my head and back.

"Evil demons, be GONE!" the aunt screamed.

"Devil's power, leave this woman NOW!" the uncle hollered.

"Ah...Will?" I asked quizzically, looking at the guy who set all this up. I don't remember exactly what I said next, but I do remember we didn't stay for dessert. Hmmmm... wonder if it was devil's food cake....

The incident really did shake me up because Christ had always been active in my life on a very personal and loving level. I was shocked that these people would so dramatically label my healing work in His name as satanic in nature. The fact that they passionately insisted THEIRS was the only true way to interpret the Bible pretty much turned me off to anyone who quoted scripture to condemn or confront, or preached exclusion and judgment. It was also my last date with *that* guy.

On the Road to Find Out

While I was surrounded by some great like-minded friends, the challenge of trying to be somewhat "normal" in a small town while constantly experiencing some pretty funky things that people in general refused to acknowledge finally got to me. I knew I had to find out once and for all if I was "psychic" or "psychotic." That meant quitting my perfectly respectable job as a national newspaper editor—the first woman in that position, and the youngest person ever—to embark on what would be a two-year spiritual quest.

It was a tough decision, and even tougher on my family. My parents were sure I had become a Moonie, and completely lost my senses. (For the younger generation, "Moonies" is the slang term for followers of Unification Church founder Sun Myung Moon, who claims to be the new Messiah.) However, I knew I could no longer pretend the spiritual realm didn't matter to me; I had to listen to my heart. My heart was making it perfectly clear that it was finally time to learn who I really was.

I packed up my sacred books and some clothes, and loaded the remnants of my old life into my orange Volkswagen Rabbit. Knowing there was no way my parents and I could have had any semblance of a rational discussion about my decision, I left without telling them when or where I was going. They arrived at my empty apartment as friends were loading up the last of the furniture, books, and dishes I had given to them. Of course, Mom and Dad were devastated that I had already left by the time they arrived. I wasn't proud of leaving like that, but I felt they left me no choice. They refused to acknowledge or respect who I was, and what I did. I had a spiritual fire burning in my heart to discover exactly how I fit into the bigger, divine scheme of things.

At that time, 12 years before this Christmas breakfast, I knew Allentown, Pennsylvania was not my home, but I didn't know what place *would* claim me as its own. My journey back to myself had started. And, I remembered, looking back at that chapter of my life, what a long, strange trip it was.

Chapter 6
The Spiritual Quest Years

From the moment my dusty little Rabbit arrived at a friend's house near the Tennessee-Georgia line, just about everything in my life changed dramatically. I went from hiding my psychic abilities to being asked to share them, constantly. Just a few weeks after arriving, I had my first foray into the world of "The Psychic Fair." For the uninitiated, a Psychic Fair is where strangers purchase 15-minute increments of your life, and you are expected to zero in accurately and instantly on their relationships, health, career path—whatever they want to discuss.

This particular Psychic Fair was in Atlanta at a spiritual center called The Foundation of Truth. Rows of card tables with a number taped to the front of each were flanked by folding chairs. Armed with tarot cards, crystal balls, pendulums, astrology charts, gauzy purple scarves, and candles, dozens of psychics were carefully setting up their tables to prepare for the eager throng gathering outside the doors.

I've never used any of the traditional trappings of professional psychics. I just do an affirmation, invoke a bubble of Christ Light, and ask God for the information that is important to the person I'm reading. I immediately start to see, hear, and feel things—past, present, and future. That morning, my sweaty hands longed for a deck of cards to clutch, a crystal ball to gaze at or *I Ching* sticks to toss. I was absolutely terrified.

The bell sounded, signaling the first wave of seekers was surging to our tables. An angry middle-aged woman stormed up to my corner of the cosmos and plunked herself down on the metal chair. "I think this whole thing is a bunch of CRAP," she spat at me, "and you have to prove to me that it's real!"

It was *so* much like the cruel ridicule of my psychic gifts I had endured from my dad growing up—but this time it was different. This woman challenged me to be authentic. She had come to me for counsel, and I had dedicated my life to being of service. I closed my eyes and silently prayed, "God, if this is what you want me to do with my life, I need a little help here!"

Suddenly, I was watching a movie in my head, and my angry client was the star. All the information she needed to know was being played out in my mind's eye. I told the woman her husband's name, and described what he looked like. I told her the names of her children, and their ages. At that point, she began to sob, and we could FINALLY get to the real reason she was there. When the bell rang again, signaling the end of the longest 15 minutes of my life, the woman tenderly hugged me, and sincerely thanked me. She looked completely transformed, peaceful, and happy. I knew she had received the validation and guidance she required to jump back into her life with joy and purpose.

So had I!

And, that's how I became a professional spiritual adviser.

Lesson of the Laughing Buddha

One of the dangers of doing this work sometimes is getting seduced by the "guru ego overload"—the old "I know best! I'm the professional psychic!" Thank goodness, I flirted with this shadow side VERY early on, and was forever put in my place by a tuned-in seven year old.

For this adventure, I was teaching a nondenominational Sunday school class at the Cosmic Church of Truth in Jacksonville, Fla. While other ministers with the Church were doing the sermons for the big people, I worked with about half a dozen children, ages four through 12. All the lessons I taught came directly from The Reliable Source.

Each Saturday evening I'd sit at my electric Smith-Corona (baffled Gen X and Y folks can Google that and learn what a "typewriter" was), do my favorite White Light affirmation to put myself in high energy, and ask God what I was supposed to teach the next morning. I'd feel the tears start to come, and then I'd pretty much just sit back and watch my fingers fly over the keyboard.

Sometimes I'd get a story, like the boy who was sailing his own ship that was named after him, and from the crow's nest he saw other ships coming toward him. At first, he was frightened and wanted to either fight or flee, but as they got closer, he realized all the other ships were under the command of his friends—and everyone's ship was named after them. It was an illustration of how everyone steers his and her own ship, and is responsible for the ship's actions.

Sometimes I'd get an activity; thankfully, I got this particular lesson a few days before class so I had time to pick up two large, commercial-sized cans of fruit. I removed the top of the cans, put the fruit into other containers, then punched two holes on either side of the bottom of both cans and threaded long shoelaces through the openings. One by one, I had the kids stand in the middle of the room and look all around. Then, I'd help them step up onto the "stilts," tie them onto their feet, and have the kids look around the room again. That lesson was showing them how their perspectives could *completely* change when they looked at the world from a higher place.

The day I got my spiritual comeuppance, I was teaching the kids about psychometry. This is the practice of picking up an object, and getting impressions such as where it came from, who owned it, what was happening at the time to the owner—all sorts of fascinating things. Because this just comes so naturally to me, I can get a bit of intuitive overload at antique shops when I forget to put up my White Light shield.

But gently refocusing… back at the Sunday school classroom, I asked several friends to lend me interesting objects I could use with the kids.

Stephen, who was four, was eager to go first. I put him in a chair in the middle of our little circle of kids and blindfolded him. Then I pressed a necklace of Egyptian mummy beads into his hand. He was so excited he could barely sit still.

"OK, Stephen, now hold on to those beads and tell me, how do you feel?"

"I feel cold," he said, which would certainly make sense since the beads had been in a pyramid.

"Good! Now what color do you see?"

"Blue!"

The beads *were* blue. He was doing great.

"One more question for you, Stephen, what shapes do you see?" I was sure he was going to say "Circles" since the beads were round. Instead, he paused a moment, then blurted out, "Triangles!"

Yikes! The kid was *seriously* good. He was seeing pyramids!

I figured three questions was about right so everyone could "play," so I removed the blindfold, took back the beads, and asked who wanted to go next. Seven-year-old Elizabeth's hand shot up first, so I nodded at her.

"Come on in here!" I told her. She scooted to the chair and plopped down. I gently wrapped the blindfold around her head, reached into my magic box, and pulled out a little statue of a Laughing Buddha a friend had lent me.

"Now, Elizabeth," I said encouragingly as I put the statue in her eager hands. "Tell us, how do you feel?"

"I feel HAPPY!" she said, giggling. We were off to a great start with the Laughing Buddha.

"Wonderful!" I encouraged her. "Listen to the little statue closely now, and tell me what kind of music you hear."

Elizabeth cocked her head as if she was hearing something from another time and space; then confidently said, "I hear all **kinds** of music!"

Did I mention I was a professional psychic? And as such, I, of course, wanted her to hear some kind of Eastern music—a gong, perhaps. A flute. Even a slow drum.

"Listen more closely, Elizabeth," I urged her. "Pay more attention, and now tell me what kind of music you can hear while you're holding that statue."

Her little face twisted into a frown.

"I hear *all kinds of music*!" she repeated, defiantly. Being the all-knowing teacher, I sighed. Poor child was doing SO well, but then just didn't have the clairaudient sensitivity for which I was looking. We ended her turn, and went on to the next excited child. About a week later, I visited my friend to return the laughing Buddha.

"I am SO glad to get this back," Ann said. "My record shelf just looks empty without it."

A cosmic brick hit me square on the head.

"Your…ah…*record shelf?*" I asked, slowly starting to turn beet red. I could swear the Buddha was laughing *very* loudly at that point.

You're the Only One

In the heart of my spiritual quest, I discovered a fantastic group—Spiritual Frontiers Fellowship (SFF). It was an eclectic organization of creative, inquisitive people who explored how the scientific and spiritual could not only co-exist, but also actually enrich each other. The group included people with careers as diverse as medical doctors and healers, priests and psychics, musicians and artists.

I attended conferences at both Guilford and Elizabethtown colleges, and delighted in the heady energy of being with like-minded souls for an entire week of learning, sharing, and discovery.

In addition to daily classes teaching such disciplines as kinesiology, spiritual dance, and raw food preparation, there were nightly speakers, concerts, discussion groups and meditations. The constant feeling of shifting and transformation was like spiritual catnip to me!

Because I had passed my intuitive reading "trial by fire" at the Foundation of Truth in Atlanta, I volunteered to be one of SFF's psychic readers at the second conference I attended. It seemed to go well, so I put my name in for the next conference, too.

I had read several people one day when a middle-aged woman came into my reading room, kicked off her sandals, and plopped down on the chair. She looked at me and smiled.

"You don't remember me, do you?" she quizzed. In all honesty, I didn't have a clue.

An aside: When I do a reading, I intentionally change the way my brain works so I can go up into an Alpha state. I go beyond my own ego, into a place of Christ Consciousness, to connect with the person—past, present and future—and retrieve the information that Spirit indicates will be most useful to him or her at this point in his or her life.

I'm more comfortable making this connection from my spiritual base, but in actuality, it also fits into purely scientific guidelines. In quantum physics, all things are interconnected on the Universal Field. When one person does an "entanglement" with another, they merge consciousness, and in theory can access each other's thoughts. It is exactly the same thing—I just prefer calling on the assistance of angels and a very tuned-in former carpenter.

But gently refocusing....

"I'm sorry," I said, smiling back at her. "I really don't remember you."

Rarely do I consciously remember the detailed information I see when I "go to level"—and rarely do I remember the particular person. It's as if God is letting me know this is *really* none of my business, and I'm just the instrument that can make the cosmic connection for the client.

"That's OK. You read me last year at the conference," she said. "I've had a *lot* of psychic readings, and you're the only one

who accurately told me what was going to happen. So let's do it again."

I breathed a silent prayer of gratitude to be doing this, at the age of 24, and helping people connect the karmic dots in their lives. I took a deep breath, and catapulted my consciousness into the Universal Field. It was flying time again!

Virginia Samdahl's Touch

In 1978, I was reading the list of classes to be offered at the SFF Guilford College Conference and stumbled on something new.

"Reiki Healing with Virginia Samdahl," I said. "What the heck is *that?*" I kept reading to learn it was Universal Life Energy, channeled through the body and the hands, and given to another person to heal body, mind, and/or spirit. Fascinating! I immediately knew that was the class I wanted. It went beyond "deciding" to take Reiki, or even "psychically seeing" I should sign up for it. It was more like Divine Knowing, when every cell in your body is standing up and cheering, "YES!" You are completely at one with the Universe, and there is such a profound yet quiet joy, and the feeling that this isn't just happy coincidence—it's destiny.

Barbara Marx Hubbard, whom I had the honor of interviewing for a cover story for the magazine *The Light Connection*, talks about the spiral of human consciousness evolution. Humanity ascends this spiral as a collective when sparked by the leadership of divinely anointed teachers. These catalysts have cracked their "cosmic eggs" —the term I love to use to talk about a person's resistance to connecting to their higher spiritual awareness—and raised their own consciousness to the point that simply by being in their presence, we, too, ascend another coil of the spiral with them.

Virginia Samdahl, a petite, sweet powerhouse of a woman, was definitely ordained to raise mass consciousness through bringing Reiki into the Western world, along with 21 other Reiki Masters initiated by Master Hawayo K. Takata of Honolulu. Virginia was the first, though, and took very seriously her responsibility to bring change and healing to the masses.

Day after day, throughout that glorious week of discovery, Virginia drilled into us the history of Reiki, the universality of its effectiveness, and the importance of our clearing ourselves as channels for this energy so we could effectively share it.

She'd walk through a maze of treatment tables, pausing to reposition a hand, quiz us on the next placement, or boost our effectiveness by placing her own hands on our backs as we worked on one another. Those hands of hers were blazing hot.

I remember her barking out orders to our class, like "Scattered fingers mean scattered energy! Keep those fingers together!"

Virginia tempered her demands with kindness and encouragement. One of the things she said, which is burned onto my heart, was, "The only difference between Christ and us is that He was born knowing He was divine, and we go to the grave denying that we are."

While she was a woman on a mission, she was also quick to laugh or share a self-deprecating story. She always reminded us we were spiritual beings in a human world, trying to remember how to be spiritual.

When she was initiating us and giving attunements, though, Virginia was much more than just human. As she stood behind me, doing the Reiki power signs in the air over my head and praying, I asked Spirit to help me be in proper alignment to receive whatever it was Virginia was preparing to share. About then, the top of my skull felt like it just flew off, and invisible bolts of lightning shot from the crown of my head out through the palms of my hands and the soles of my feet, linking me forever to the earth while simultaneously giving me wings to fly. As always when I transition to another level of awareness, my tears flowed freely.

The week zipped by, and I was sad to leave this Midwestern avatar. Virginia and I had developed a special bond, and she told me I was going to go on to do great things with both Reiki, and with my spiritual gifts. I interviewed her for a story for the now-defunct magazine, *Psychic Dimensions*. You can read the entire article in the back of this book.

Meeting Jim Goure

At an SFF Conference, it wasn't just the scheduled events that were such a draw, but also the excitement of meeting others on the same path. It was during a 1979 conference I met a man who would definitely change the course of my life almost as much as Virginia Samdahl had.

Jim Goure was one of those marvelous conundrums—a scientist who, in his mature years, went mystical. Jim was a graduate of the U.S. Naval Academy, served as a Commander in the post-WW II Navy, and ended up with the Atomic Energy Commission in Washington, D.C. He shared a story of how he received a huge spiritual epiphany when the atom was split and revealed a core of pure light. He said it was at that moment he realized the true core of *everything* was light.

After his retirement, he set about creating a Light Center, where he could further explore the powerful, healing effect different kinds of light could have on people. He also wanted to share his *Seven Steps to Effective Prayer* with others, and envisioned creating a 24-hour prayer network. His intent was that at any time of the day or night, people would be praying for peace. He felt it was a necessary move to offset the atrocities of the atom bomb.

Jim and I were united by the same birthday (though in very different decades!) and an irreverent, quick sense of humor. He was so impressed with the reading I gave him at SFF he invited me to come be the resident psychic—and newsletter editor—at his new United Research Light Center in Black Mountain, North Carolina.

I was honored and thrilled with the invitation, and accepted. My carrot-orange VW Rabbit stretched its legs to hop up the steep, winding mountain roads and deliver me to 55 Star Route. As the pink quartz in the heart of these ancient hills started to connect with me, I was drawn into the power and healing of this sacred place.

Towering regiments of pine trees blocked huge chunks of sky, and the dense, moist energy of the thick woods hinted at the magic and mystery that was to make itself known to me. I was home—at least for this chapter in my life.

Winged Welcome

The summer evening I arrived, Jim welcomed me warmly and introduced me to his lovely wife, and the three of his eight children who still lived at home. I also met the other members of the team—an eclectic collection of eight women and men, young and old, who lived at the lodge and dedicated themselves to being of service, and bringing into reality Jim's visions of prayer and peace through light.

I learned that we prayed four times a day (little bells signaled the prayer times), and each of us would have specific duties for a week at a time. We could sign up to cook the meals, clean the lodge, haul wheelbarrows full of gravel to the steep roads leading up to the house and down to the construction site for the domed Light Center—any one of many jobs, all important to the growth and development of United Research.

It was quite a lot to take in, and I was only too happy to retire to a room and zonk out after dinner that first night. I was SO ready for a deep, peaceful sleep, but Spirit had other plans. No sooner had I entered into a light slumber than a huge entity with black, leathery wings swooped from a corner of the room and flew right at my neck. I immediately invoked the Prayer of Protection and Christ Light and banished the creature, then prayed the *hell* out of that room. After I had energetically cleared it, I was finally able to fall asleep.

The next morning, Jim was cheerfully flipping pancakes as I walked into the kitchen.

"What the *heck* was that thing in my room last night?" I demanded.

Jim gave me a huge grin. "We were wondering if you were going to notice that," he admitted, a bit guiltily. "A woman who stayed in the room before you had quite a few problems and we hadn't completely 'cleaned' everything out of there."

We definitely weren't in Kansas anymore!

God is the Center of it All

When I arrived at the Light Center, the domed prayer, meditation and education structure itself was just starting to materialize from the rolls of architectural drawings. The wooden framework for the cement foundation was in place, and a web of pipes and wires spanned the yet-to-be-poured foundation. Smack in the center was a short open pipe. The cement truck was due the next morning, and I received a spiritual "directive" of what I was to do before it arrived.

That evening, after the site had been deserted for the night, I walked back down the gravel road and stood looking at the promontory that would soon be home to this international prayer center. I reached into my pocket and pulled out a small piece of paper and a pen. After writing the word, "GOD," on the paper, I folded it, blessed it, and dropped it into the pipe in the center of the foundation. By the time I faithfully greeted the "Angel of Mid-Morning" upon arising around 9:30 a.m. the following day, the cement truck had already visited, forever sealing God as the center of everything at the United Research Light Center. God is good!

A Lot to Learn

The Light Center construction moved into high gear after the foundation was poured, and soon the arc of the geodesic dome rose from the circle that held the round Light Room. In the very center of the sacred space, right over "God," banks of theatrical lights flanked the Light Room, and a circle of red armless chairs joined together to create a round "sofa."

The room was configured that way so people could sit in the red chairs and one by one, every five minutes, the colors of light shining on them would move up the rainbow spectrum.

First, you would have five minutes of just red light shining on you. Then, five minutes of orange, followed by five minutes each of yellow, green, and so on. An audio system delivered appropriate music, usually either a calming instrumental piece or chanting, as you received your cleansing "light bath."

The sacred energy coming from that space was evident to all who experienced it, and from its official opening in October 1979, miraculous healings began to happen.

Being the resident psychic, and also doing my fair share of the chores, was a lot of work, but one of the perks was being able to meditate and pray for hours on end in the upstairs domed Prayer Room.

It was during one of my marathon out of body adventures that I had another one of those consciousness expanding visions. Maybe it really happened. It's hard to say. Anyway, I became aware of a humanoid creature sitting in full lotus position in one of the triangular windows in the Dome. The appearance of the thing startled me—it had a huge head, spindly arms and legs, huge eyes, and taupe-colored textured skin. I immediately invoked the Prayer of Protection and Christ Light.

Suddenly, Jesus was there in all His glory, with brilliant white and golden light emanating from His face and robes. He moved right past me to bow His head at the creature, and the two of them exchanged blessings. It was obvious they had a deep, abiding connection. Then, He turned to me.

"You have a lot to learn about light," He said simply but kindly, and then vanished in a flash of gold.

WHOA! What had just happened? It took me a moment to realize, but Christ Himself had let me know that just because an entity looks different certainly doesn't mean it's not of the Light. It was a humbling, powerful lesson, and one I've never forgotten. It also put out the fascinating thought that Extra-terrestrials—if that's what this strange creature was—can have a deep spiritual connection to Christ just like us Earthlings.

The next day was Thanksgiving, and multiple tables were assembled in the living and dining rooms to accommodate the overflow of friends and family. I was sitting at Jim's table and shared the vision with him, and he promptly stood up, silenced all the other conversations, and made me repeat the story. Let me tell you, it was equally humbling that time, too.

It wasn't until years later I heard the Hopi stories about a tribe of people who chose to go underground to survive the last Ice Age, and remain a thriving culture today in their subterranean world. I got a jolt of electricity, and realized I had probably seen one of these Hopi Elders exchanging sacred greeting with Jesus.

Or else an alien visitor to Earth.

Or maybe, they're the same thing....

You Are Here

In the first few years of the Light Center's existence, a wooden equilateral cross with a globe of the Earth in the center marked the outside entrance to the lower floor, where the Light Room waited. The globe, encased in a clear plastic window, was about eight inches in diameter and slowly revolved, putting every nation in light as it turned on its axis.

Never one to resist an opportunity to help people take themselves less seriously, one night I crept down to the Dome and did a little extra decorating. The next morning, as Jim watched the globe revolve, he doubled over laughing when a tiny "You are here" flag appeared in the Western North Carolina area of the Earth.

And, the darndest thing was that he immediately knew who had added that flag. Humor was always my way of deflecting fear or judgment from people who were uncomfortable with my psychic ability—but it was also a great way to celebrate the joy and connection we share on our spiritual journey. Truly, where there is laughter, there is God.

Releasing the Past

Although I've had very strong past life recall since I was a child, intellectually, I'm still not convinced that we each literally have a string of bodies littered around the globe from different lifetimes. What I strongly believe is that we can—either intentionally or through divine intervention—energetically connect with another time, place, and person. In other words, if all time exists simultaneously, all we have to do is raise our brain waves to reach that point of interconnectedness, and we can link to Joan of Arc, or Geronimo, or Socrates, or a humble shepherd in Wales in the 15th century. It's all accessible to us when we release the idea of limitations, separations, and chronological time.

That being said, occasionally when I'm reading a person, I'll get a VERY clear message about a specific "past" life. Sometimes, I'll be looking at the person and as I focus on his or her eyes, the rest of the face and body fade away, and a new person with the same eyes appears. Even the eyes can change size, shape, and color, but the essence, the energetic soul visible through the eyes, remains constant. In all cases, the information I receive has a literal parallel to something happening in the person's life right now.

Being able to reference a past life lets people access the lessons and wisdom learned from past behaviors without being "judged" for what they're doing in this lifetime.

Speaking of judgment, a quick tangent: I was reading a pleasant, very intuitive young woman, and she was quite upset with her tendency to be extremely judgmental of others. It was impacting her personal and professional life in a negative way, and she was trying unsuccessfully to figure out where this was coming from.

I "went up" to get more information, and froze—"she" became a "he," and instantly was transformed into one of the Puritanical judges from the Salem Witch Trials. But the *really* freaky part was that "he" was pointing at *me*, and condemning me to death for being a witch. I had gone back in time with her and discovered we shared an experience in which she had sentenced me to death for my spiritual abilities.

Now, in this lifetime, she was struggling with accepting her own highly advanced spiritual gifts, particularly because she had judged others so harshly for theirs. When I shared this information with her, she was horrified, but slowly began to connect the dots and see how she could transform her current life with this new knowledge from the past. Karma can be a bitch, no? But karmic wisdom is profoundly healing.

Now, gently refocusing....

One young couple who had been frequent Light Center guests visited while I was living there, and this time they were engaged. The man had been told in numerous psychic readings that he'd been a pharaoh in a past life, and loved the prestige that honor afforded him now. He also loved being read, and asked me to do a session for him. I did, and quickly saw that ancient Egyptian lifetime of power, riches, and infallibility. That made him quite happy.

He was not happy, though, with what I was told to convey to him—that this lifetime a big part of his mission was to release whom he *had* been to concentrate on whom he was *now*. If he held on to his past, it would prevent him from fully living his mission for his current incarnation.

After I completed his reading, I asked his fiancée if she also wanted a session. She was very sweet, and thanked me, but said she didn't feel the need for a reading. I told her I completely understood, and that was that.

Fast-forward a dozen years, and I'm the broadcast publicity supervisor at Disneyland. I open up one Sunday's *Parade Magazine* to discover the cover story is "Spirituality in America." Fascinated, I begin reading, and then stop. There's a picture of a smiling woman I recognize as the man's fiancée. In the caption, though, she had his last name, indicating they had indeed married.

She was an important part of the story because she had been recognized as the incarnation of a female Dalai Lama, and Buddhist monks and nuns from around the world made pilgrimages to the couple's New Jersey home to pay homage to her.

I laughed out loud—and sincerely hoped the man had managed to release his past life to make room for hers. A Dalai Lama trumps a pharaoh ANY day!

Psychic Shopping

One of the times I signed on to be the lodge grocery go-fer, I picked up the weekly shopping list from the guy doing the cooking and made the long trip to the only grocery store in the area in 1979. Richard, a professional chef on his own spiritual quest, had meticulously listed all the items he needed to make the meals for the next seven days.

I located all the requested ingredients and was pushing the loaded shopping cart toward the checkout line when I suddenly heard the word, "Cabbage!" I immediately turned the cart around and trudged back to the produce section to get several heads of cabbage.

At the point I was almost back in the checkout line, I distinctly heard, "Raisins!" Again, I turned the cart around, found the raisin aisle, and grabbed a large box.

As I pulled into the driveway of the lodge with a trunk full of groceries, Richard opened the door and grinned at me. "Did you get my message? I decided to make stuffed cabbage with raisins, too," he said.

The fact that we could literally mentally merge across the miles, long before cell phones existed, proves more to me about quantum physics than any scientific theory ever could. And, the most exciting part about the experience for me was that it all felt quite comfortable and, dare I say, logical, too.

Flying Psychologist

During my time as resident psychic at the Light Center, a psychologist from Michigan, let's rename him "Andrew," visited to collect information for research he was conducting into the dynamics of spiritual communities. I was something of a unique case—a psychic who also had a background as a professional news journalist—so Andrew invited me to go out and discuss what it was like being at United Research.

We went to a restaurant down the mountain and in the nearby city of Asheville, and were seated at the bar until a table became available.

"So what's it like to be psychic?" the good doctor asked.

"Well, it's a spiritual calling," I explained as we perched on the bar stools, "but it can also be a lot of fun. For instance, watch those banana slices the bartender just put on those daiquiris," I instructed him.

Just for the record, I pretty much stopped doing the "parlor tricks" part of telepathy and telekinesis after college, but this guy was such a clinical type that I thought he needed to loosen up a bit. Andrew turned to look at the drinks, and one of the banana slices fell off the glass and onto the counter.

"Did... did YOU...?"

I pointed back to the glasses, and he turned in time to see the other banana slide off the second glass.

His eyes like saucers, he stared at both fallen bananas, then back at me. Andrew's strict clinical training was starting to fall apart.

Later, back at the lodge, he was still puzzling over what he had seen, but was also feeling strangely drawn to me.

I was taught that both spiritual and sexual energy emanate from the first chakra, the energy center in the body that's located at the base of the spine. Frequently people will think they're feeling a sensual pull to someone when what they're actually sensing is a spiritual connection. That's why people think they're falling in love with their ministers, for instance.

Anyway, I knew that Andrew was reacting to my spiritual energy, and right about then he started coming toward me with his arms out. I knew he was going to hug me, and it didn't feel right to me. I just remember thinking, "No."

Suddenly Andrew was thrown three feet back against the wall. I hadn't moved a muscle. He stood there, arms splayed against the paneling, mouth gaping. Watching a banana slice fall from a glass was ONE thing. Feeling himself being flung against a wall by an invisible force he had never experienced and could not explain, despite his clinical training, was quite another. Andrew left the lodge shortly after that, and I never DID hear if he wrote about any of his experiences during his visit.

After that dramatic evening, I've never thrown anyone else against a wall. But, I like to think that if I ever really *needed* to....

The Hurricane

Shortly after the Light Center opened its doors to the world, a tropical storm began building off the coast of Miami. As it continued to grow in strength and fury, it appeared a full-blown massive hurricane was going to make a direct strike on the city. If it did, the consequences to both Miami and the entire Eastern seaboard would be catastrophic.

Five of us gathered in one of the basement bedrooms at the lodge and began to pray, putting the city and the whole region in an industrial-strength bubble of white light. We visualized the hurricane suddenly changing course, and veering back out to the open sea, where it dissipated.

We'll never know if it was the combined energy of the countless people who were also praying for Miami, or divine intervention, or both, but the hurricane ended up doing exactly what we were visualizing. Miami only received a steady rain shower. In addition, we received the gift of knowing that when a situation seems hopeless, just stop everything and pray. It truly is the most powerful thing you can do, particularly when your own prayers connect with those of others.

Plugging In To Practical Spirituality

After about eight months at the Light Center, I was growing increasingly uncomfortable with the fact that people for whom I did intuitive consultations started to put me on a pedestal.

Instead of seeing me as a resource to help them connect with their higher self, people saw me as the "Answer Guru."

Concerned, I refused to take up that role, and said to God in an intense meditation in the Dome, "ANYONE can do readings like I'm doing!" Clear as a bell, a deep voice responded, "So teach them how!"

Startled, I asked, "Ah...how exactly do I DO that?" That's when I received an extremely detailed, step-by-step instruction in how to guide people to the infinite wisdom they carry within.

Although I grew up extremely sensitive and it was just second nature to me, the contents of the class I got from The Reliable Source seemed too simple to work. It was just guided meditations, putting together the meanings of various colors, symbols, and images, praying, and then...well...doing a reading.

Two women from Pennsylvania were visiting the Light Center when I received my "divine download" for the class, and I asked them if they'd like to take the first class, and be my guinea pigs. They were only too delighted.

Sure enough, it really WAS that simple. By the time we were through, in just a few hours, both women were amazing themselves and me by doing accurate, detailed readings for each other as well as people from the lodge I pulled in to give the women more practice.

I realized the class, which I decided to call "Practical Spirituality 101," worked because of two key things. First of all, people aren't normally told they can do this, and there's usually a stigma attached to anything "unusual." When it becomes not only OK, but required, to start intuitively connecting the dots, everyone can.

Secondly, as humanity continues up that evolutionary spiral we talked about earlier, abilities that were once considered "rare" become more common, and the social zeitgeist reflects the shift. Just consider what spiritual concepts movies are exposing people to in popular flicks like *Avatar*, the *Star Wars*, *Harry Potter* and *Lord of the Rings* series, *Close Encounters*, *ET*, *The Philadelphia Experiment*, *Whale Rider*, *The*

Sixth Sense, What the Bleep Do We Know and *The Secret*, along with so many others.

Even television is raising consciousness and expanding people's ideas of what's possible. Shows like *Roswell, Star Trek, Medium, Ghost Whisperer, New Amsterdam, Quantum Leap, Joan of Arcadia, Wonderfalls, Dead Like Me* and tons more are the contemporary equivalent of Original Peoples' "storytellers," the ones who share the tribe's history and legends, and make people strive to savor all life has to offer. These stories connect us to our past and can launch us into our future with our eyes—all three of them, counting that psychic Third Eye in the middle of everyone's forehead—wide open.

I've been teaching Practical Spirituality 101 ever since I received it that night more than 30 years ago, praying by myself in the Dome, illumined only by the light of the stars shining through the windows in the roof. Moreover, of course, because this class didn't come FROM me, but only THROUGH me, it always, always works. I never cease to be overwhelmed with gratitude and humility that I can help so many others add sacred dimensions to their lives.

Moving On

I was at the Light Center for less than a year, but learned, or "remembered," several lifetimes' worth of important information during my time there. Jim was a friend, mentor, challenger, inspiration, and occasional royal pain, frequently simultaneously. I am forever grateful to him for opening his heart, his home, and his dream to me.

I was starting to get dreams and visions, though, gently telling me it was time to get back into the real world and teach my truths by living them. I was getting glimpses of my future, and I had a lot of work to do that was going to take me around the globe. I packed up my VW again and drove into the next chapter of my life.

Chapter 7

Back in the 'Real World'

Even though I had no background in television, I had solid print news journalist roots. That, combined with holding the strong intent that I *would* be hired, landed me a job at a TV station in Asheville in the mountains of Western North Carolina. Even though I'd been a hotshot national editor at the newspaper, switching from print to broadcast journalism meant I had to start at the bottom of the food chain again. I was hired as a "news writer," which meant I got everyone's dinner and wrote stories from the wires as assigned by the 11 p.m. producer.

I was still living at United Research Light Center in Black Mountain, so I had an hour-long commute to the TV station. Bridgette Erdman Berthiez, a woman who frequently attended events at the Light Center, had become a good friend, and she invited me to house-sit for her in Asheville while she visited her native Germany for the summer. She was offering me kind of a halfway house in my transition from living in a spiritual community on a mountain to coming back down into the real world.

Bridgette was brilliant, funny, powerful, and beautiful. She told heart-wrenching stories about growing up in Germany during the war, and how her feet were crippled because her family couldn't afford to buy new shoes as the children's feet grew. Her home was a charming, eclectic mix of old-world tradition and New Age funky.

Bridgette invited me to move into the finished basement family room the week before she left for Europe so I could get used to the house while she was still there. That first night, I had just turned off the light and snuggled under the covers when I felt a cool breeze. I opened my eyes to see an aristocratic old woman floating over the bed. Her steel gray hair was swept back from her temples, and she had a thin, angular nose.

Now, please understand that even if you grow *up* seeing spirit visitors, as I did, it can still be a bit intense when they decide to come chat if you are not expecting them. I yanked the covers over my head and took a deep breath. Invoking the white light, I steeled myself and slowly poked my head back out. Sure enough, the distinguished looking woman was still floating there, regarding me kind of impatiently. She gave me some information, then slowly dissolved away.

I reached over to turn on the bedside lamp, and failed at my repeated attempts to fall asleep. The second I heard Bridgette's footsteps the next morning, I leaped out of bed and raced up the stairs toward the kitchen.

"Do you know a thin woman with long gray hair and a pointy nose?" I asked breathlessly.

"Oh, just a minute," Bridgette said in her delightfully thick accent. She disappeared into her bedroom and came back into the kitchen cradling a framed photograph. "Is this her?"

"YES!" I answered.

"This was my Aunt…."

I couldn't wait for her to finish the sentence. "She said the furniture is coming," I blurted out.

"Oh, no," Brigitte corrected me. "When she died her estate was tied up. It will take the courts years to finally settle everything."

Of course the call from Germany came in the next few days—the estate rather miraculously became untangled, and her aunt's exquisite furniture was soon Asheville-bound, to Bridgette's delight.

I, on the other hand, would have been delighted if the aunt had just gone *up* one flight of stairs to talk directly with Bridgette in the first place!

Melting Pot

After Bridgette returned from Germany and I needed to find a new place to live, a friend and fellow reporter at the station and I decided to rent a little house together. We got along quite well even though we were very different. While she had cute plush bunnies hugging one another in her room, I had a spaceship suspended from the ceiling light in mine.

At Christmas, she spent a fun evening at her parents' place across town and came back to our house all excited.

"Guess what my folks got me!" she said.

I looked at her for a minute then responded, "An electric fondue pot."

She stopped dead in her tracks, staring at me with dinner-plate-sized eyes. I kept looking at her. "Yellow," I added. At that point, she screamed and ran out of the room. Eventually, after I'd made some jokes about the incident, she was fine and we just didn't dwell on it. However, I did resolve to be a bit more subtle in the future.

Psychic Promotion

While I had accepted the news writer job at the TV station to get my toe in the door, I aspired to have more of a say about what kind of information was actually put into the newscasts. Since I had *no* background in broadcast journalism, I focused on watching everything that was going on to absorb all the information I could, and I even meditated in the ladies' lounge during dinner breaks. The potential power to do good with TV news fascinated and inspired me.

Four months after I was first hired, I had my opportunity. The 11 p.m. producer called in sick, and I took her call. On the spur of the moment, I decided that instead of telling the News Director the woman wasn't coming in to do the show, *I'd* produce the newscast. I knew I'd either be fired or promoted. My psychic sense was feeling more of the latter.

As I was planning the stories for the newscast, I called on my intuitive ability, and remember feeling everything just starting to flow. I "knew" who would be available for interviews. I "knew" what video we had in the library, and what we would need to shoot. I even "knew" to leave a blank space in the first block for a major story that hadn't happened yet—but was going to in the next hour. And, it did.

Bottom line—I was in the zone, and the next day was promoted to full-time 11 p.m. producer. And that's the true story of how I moved into TV management.

Auto Suggestion

One wintry Western North Carolina evening, my date and I were on our way to dinner in my Volkswagen Rabbit. I was driving.

Suddenly the car in the lane to my right hit a patch of black ice and started spinning toward us.

"Bubble up!" I yelled at the guy, which was my shorthand version of the All-Purpose Affirmation in the front of this book. The affirmation invokes a sphere of powerful white light around you, protecting you from unwanted things coming into your energetic field.

The other car skidded to within a foot of my car, then looked as if it "hit" an invisible, intangible something, straightened out, and slid back into its correct lane. There was no crunching metal, squealing tires, or sign of any kind of impact—other than that apparent bounce off an invisible energy field that safely enveloped the Rabbit.

"What the heck just happened?" my date asked, ashen-faced.

"We used the force," I said. "It's quite real, you know."

I vaguely remember it was a very short date.

Footnotes

I have Pisces rising and a major configuration in Cancer, which means I'm fine-tuned to be a healer and nurturer. One day shortly after I was promoted to producer at the TV station, I arrived at work to see one of the young reporters, Deborah Potter, wincing in pain as she tried to straighten out her neck.

"What happened?" I asked her.

"I think I slept on my neck funny," she said.

"Sit down and take off your shoes," I said reflexively. Debbie looked surprised but did as I told her. I sat down in a chair facing her and took one of her feet in my hands. I immediately started massaging the base of the big toe, which, in foot reflexology, corresponds to the neck. I had studied the Mildred Carter method of the modality for several years. Within seconds, her neck popped back into alignment and her head straightened into a normal position.

"You're a WITCH!" Debbie said, starting to draw back in fear.

I remembered, a bit too late, that many people weren't overly eager to embrace new healing concepts. She eventually did mellow out after I made a few self-deprecating jokes, but I learned the importance of *asking* someone if they wanted help before just diving in. It was an essential lesson to learn.

New Boss

Television newsrooms are a huge game of musical chairs, and there's a running joke that there are only 40 people in the industry—we just keep changing stations. About a year after I joined WLOS a new news director came in, and his first day there happened to be an election night.

By this time, I'd been promoted to the producer of the 6 p.m. newscast, and I was stacking the show, or writing in the order of the stories for the newscast, when he approached my desk.

"Let me see what you've got," he said, and I handed the worksheet to him.

He regarded it for a moment, furrowed his brow, then handed it back to me.

"That's not quite right," he said. "I want to think about it, and I'll let you know what to change."

I tuned in to him as he walked away, and "felt" how he thought. I erased several of the stories and moved them around to reflect his preferences.

When he returned to my desk a few minutes later, he reached down and picked up the revamped rundown. "Now what I want you to do…" he began confidently then he stopped. His eyes got bigger as he stared at the paper. He cleared his throat, returned the sheet to my desk, and turned to walk away again. "That's right," is all he said.

Dream Job

After three years at WLOS I'd been promoted to executive news producer at the TV station, and I'd been "discovered" by a television consultant who eventually created Audience Research and Development, a nationally respected media strategy consulting company based in Dallas. He was using my "psychically produced" newscasts to show other TV stations what they should be doing.

While that was gratifying, I was ready to shift from straight news into news promotion, which I felt was a heck of a lot more fun. The head honchos didn't want me to leave the company, so they offered me a promotion producer position at their TV station in Miami. I jumped at the chance. I was completely switching careers again, and was getting into something for which I'd never trained. But, then again, I knew how to use "The Force!" Within four months, by staying psychically tuned in, I'd won my first regional Addy award, the advertising industry's equivalent of the Emmy. I was in the flow.

I loved the fast-paced, creative energy of the job, and swiftly rose up the ranks to become the manager of the Advertising and Promotions department.

To me, everything is an opportunity to make the world a better place somehow, and that even applied to television advertising. To that end, I was puzzling over a particular project that presented me with a unique opportunity to really raise awareness. A reporter was producing a special report on how children could easily confuse fantasy and reality when they watched TV. It was a serious issue, and I was determined to create a compelling, proactive promotion that would captivate people's interest, and entice them into watching the show.

I agonized over finding just the right images and words to convey the importance of the theme. As is always the case when we try to force something, I couldn't come up with anything. Nada. Zilch. Tapping into higher consciousness happens best when you just release yourself to the cosmic flow.

After several days of dead ends, I finally surrendered one night. As I was falling asleep, I simply said, "OK, God, a little help here, please. This one's important!" Almost immediately I fell into a deep sleep, and then I saw it. The entire promotional spot, complete with very detailed animation and sound effects, appeared to me in a lucid dream state. I forced myself to wake up, and grabbed the pencil and tablet I kept by the bed. Furiously I scribbled it all down—the words I heard, and the pictures I saw. Then I fell back asleep.

The next morning, I timed the copy from my nocturnal transcription. It took exactly 29 seconds to read, the perfect length for the promotional spot. Next, I whipped out the storyboard, specifying each multi-layered effect.

When I got to the control room for my production session, my director was there waiting for me. The young man had enormous talent, and an ego to match. I handed him my very detailed storyboard.

He stared at it for a few seconds, flipping through the pages. Then he looked over at me and cocked his eyebrows.

"Where does this stuff come to you?" He asked in a less-than-friendly tone. "In DREAMS?"

I choked back the laughter and tried to keep a poker face.

"That's funny," I answered, and we dove in. Throughout the next few hours I had him do edits and special effects several times, until they were EXACTLY as I'd seen them the previous night. The director was livid, but followed my requests to the letter. It was a tense session, but the finished spot was absolutely the right tone to convey the socially responsible message.

Besides garnering us a fantastic audience for the show the night it aired, the spot earned BOTH of us Emmy recognition. I never told him it actually DID come to me in a dream…

Tough Ed-ucation

While I was learning the broadcasting promotion business in Miami, my spirit guides were teeing me up for a series of major life lessons. After a year of spreading my wings in the marvelous, magical energy of Miami and loving my life at the TV station, a new news director we've been calling "Ed" in this memoir arrived at the station to shake things up. Yes, *that* Ed. The one I married, and then was literally dying to get away from. But since you're this far into the book, you already know that.

A quick recap—the year after Ed and I married in Miami we moved to Wichita, Kansas, for the tough life-lesson adventure detailed in the first two chapters. I "died," we divorced, I searched for a job that would take me *out* of Ed's life, and put me back on my spiritual path.

So we can tee up for the "Camelot" period of my life, when my knight in shining armor arrived to sweep me into his arms and ride with me into the glorious sunshine of openly using my intuitive abilities. Of course, to tell this part of the story, we will soon be traveling to The Happiest Place on Earth, and start wishing on those stars….

Chapter 8
A Mickey Mouse Life

From the moment I arrived back in Wichita after my reflective Christmas break in Allentown, Ed was on a mission to get me the *heck* out of there ASAP. I was a daily reminder to him, and the rest of the team, of his transgressions. His life got even more complicated when I told him I psychically knew he and his mistress had traveled to Chicago so his minister brother could marry them. I'm not sure which part of that scared him more—the fact that I intuitively knew what he'd done, or the fact that I now had the courage to tell him I knew. Thanks to the new clarity I had after the holiday trip back to my hometown, the dynamic between Ed and me shifted dramatically. This did not make him a happy camper.

As eager as he was to have me leave, I was even more eager to go. I just had to find a magical solution to my job search. I was looking for that fairy tale solution.

Heigh Ho, Heigh Ho!

Like all kids growing up in the 60s, I knew Sunday evening was reserved for Walt Disney's Wonderful World of Color. The trauma of trooping back to school early Monday morning was made more bearable knowing that I'd get to spend an hour with Walt and his marvelous creations the night before.

Whether it was exploring the frontier with Davy Crocket or spotting all 101 Dalmatians, I knew I was going to have a ball parked in front of the TV.

Walt was warm, funny, caring, and smart—it was as if Central Casting cooked up the ideal "Grandpa" archetype and put him on the screen to reassure everyone the world truly was a wonderful, whimsical, magical carousel of color and fun.

After my nasty divorce, when a friend told me Disneyland was looking for someone with broadcast news experience for their Public Relations department, I was all ears. I threw my hat in the ring, and pretty soon the Mouse House flew me from Wichita, Kansas to Anaheim, California for an interview. I instantly adored Disneyland PR Manager Greg Albrecht, and our meetings went great. Not so great was the timing. The Walt Disney Company was just launching some major initiatives, and Greg was tied up in endless meetings. He was unable to get back to me right away.

Realizing he had to know up-front about my wacko sense of humor, I decided to take the initiative. He had mentioned he had two young sons, so I sent them two kids' T-shirts with the Kansas TV station's logo on them, along with a note that read something like: "Hey, kids! Wouldn't it be great if your dad didn't have to worry so much about work, and he could spend more time at home with you having fun? Just wear these shirts all the time and you can help make that happen!"

Greg called to let me know his sons refused to take the shirts off, even wearing them to bed. He said he was so sorry, but wasn't able to make a move until after some additional upcoming corporate meetings. Meanwhile, my time at the station, working for Ed, was becoming unbearable.

So, two weeks later, I cut up some newspaper headlines and, letter by letter, pasted together a one-sheet message, which I FedExed to Greg with no additional enclosure. This note read:

"We got your mouse. Call Jonna Rae RIGHT NOW or next we're sending you a BIG ROUND EAR!"

He called the next day, laughing hysterically, and just as I had seen, he offered me the job. I officially became a senior public relations representative and Disney cast member—the company's term for employees.

As quickly as you can say, "Supercalifragilisticexpialidocious," I packed up my Kansas life, bid a tearful farewell to Elma and some other close friends there, and headed west.

For a gal who grew up seeing sparks flying off of people and catching glimpses of fairies in the trees, being in a real place where a prefabricated magical environment was the norm was WILD. I would walk by a conference room and see Cinderella and Peter Pan sitting around the table with "mortal" managers. During lunch breaks I could catch a quick Star Wars flight to Endor. The Haunted Mansion? Folks, there really ARE ghosts in there. More on that later! And a cruise on the Mark Twain was a quick time-travel trip into a kinder, gentler America. It was fantastic.

One Good One Left

There were some other great people in the Public Relations department besides Greg then, too, many of whom are still friends today. One of them, Pamela Espinosa, was an assistant to Greg. I started at the Park in June, and she and I decided to go see *Terminator 2* on the 4th of July. During dinner afterwards, our conversation of course turned to guys. Pam shared that she had recently split from her husband.

"I think all men are pond scum," I said with conviction. Then I shared the drama of my recent near-death experience, and Ed's subsequent betrayal and divorce.

"Well, there's one good one left," Pam said. She was referring to her brother Paul Lankford, a Disneyland "lifer" who had survived his own unpleasant divorce a few years earlier. Pam introduced us, and there were instant fireworks. He was tall, handsome, sweet, smart, and kind to everyone.

If you visited Disneyland before December of 2000, chances are you met Paul as he served up sundaes at Carnation Restaurant on Main Street in the 70s, or worked on the Steam Trains, Big Thunder Mountain, The Mark Twain Steamboat, or other attractions at the Park. Paul absolutely loved his job. He was the epitome of a people-person—outgoing, a quick sense of humor, solution-oriented, and, above all, truly joyful. When he encountered exhausted parents yelling at rambunctious kids, he would defuse a tense family situation by making everyone laugh. He so enjoyed his close contact with people that shortly after he was promoted to a supervisory position, he asked to go back to working on the front line. The part-time job he started in high school and college became his life.

In addition to being a model Disney employee, Paul was a loyal friend, the one everyone went to when they had any kind of a problem. He was the most spiritual man I ever met, even though he didn't have any kind of formal religious beliefs. He just lived his spirituality. He honored his family, his friends, everyone. His favorite Mark Twain quote was, "If you never lie, you never have to remember what you told anybody." That's a pretty good indicator of what Paul was all about.

For the first time, I was approaching a relationship as *equals*; Paul wasn't controlling, judgmental or manipulative. Instead, he was caring, tender, funny, affectionate, and respectful of both my spiritual beliefs, *and* my psychic ability, which I brought up immediately. I had broken the cycle! I had found a twin flame, and the light shining off of him, and us together, was glorious.

In fact, our first date lasted 13 hours because we couldn't stop talking with each other! We had so much in common, and we both knew that first evening together, we were eventually going to end up married. Since I was still emotionally healing from the nasty divorce from Ed, I was absolutely terrified at the prospect of marrying again. Paul just smiled and said, "I can wait." And, he did.

From the moment I met him, despite the immediate happy fireworks, there was a faint shadow over our relationship, even though I didn't consciously know why. I was always telling Paul to put sun block on his lips. When we married, I didn't take his last name, and I never put him as the beneficiary on any of my papers. He found this a bit odd, but it was never that big a thing to him.

As we were to learn a decade later, our glorious time together was going to be tragically cut short. In the moment, though, our lives immediately intertwined in love, laughter and an easy intimacy that restored my faith, trust, and respect in the male of the species. It was as though in the great cosmic scheme of things, I wasn't to be Paul's "psychic," but just his loving mate. For now....

Enter Walt!

As I was getting into the swing of shifting into a Disney frame of mind, Walt was getting ready to introduce himself. I didn't have too long to wait.

Just a few weeks into my new life and new career at the Happiest Place on Earth, one night in my sleep a perfectly idyllic dream shifted gears, and all the colors changed to stark shades of gray. Walt himself charged into the middle of the "stage" that suddenly appeared in my nocturnal adventure.

"Just what the HELL is wrong with all the marketing people?" he demanded, slamming his fist down on the desk that just appeared in front of him. "Is EVERYONE'S head up their ass?"

His eyes were glassy; that perfectly slicked back hair erupted in unruly spikes, and blue veins bulged on his forehead. I thought I could smell alcohol on his breath as he leaned closer to yell at me.

"AND WHEN DID WOMEN START THINKING THEY COULD RUN THINGS?"

I was shocked and speechless. This raging tyrant certainly wasn't the kindly Walt Disney I knew growing up! Somehow this dream was completely out of whack. The tirade continued, though, with this "Nasty Walt" outlining specific things he wanted Marketing to be focusing on. Immediately! And, just as quickly as he stormed into my dream, he was gone.

When I awoke the next morning, I quickly jotted down the things Walt was demanding. I typed them up as proposals after I got to work, and handed them off to Greg.

"Wow," he said, looking through the pages. "Where did THIS come from?"

"Ah…you know…I was just thinking about the history of the park, and got a few ideas," I said vaguely. It was waayyyyy too early to start talking about the way I experienced life!

"I'll take these to the corporate planning meeting in Orlando," Greg said.

Two main things you have to know. First, Walt's demands were adopted and executed. Second, I later learned from people who had actually worked with Walt that the wildly inappropriate, angry man I met in the dream was the real Walt Disney. Brilliant, creative, driven, and a true visionary—yes; and also, all that other nasty stuff.

Walt continued to feed me ideas during my five years with Disney. One of my favorites was the Disney Youth Citizenship Competition, which challenged eighth graders to work within established systems to address challenging issues in students' lives. Walt showed me THAT one on a Saturday my husband and I were sailing our catamaran off Newport Beach. Even in spirit, Walt did NOT believe in taking weekends off.

I wrote up the proposal and gave it to my enthusiastic boss, who immediately started working to move the idea up the Disney food chain. It soon caught the attention, and the approval of, the upper echelon.

Disney did a test run with the concept, putting it in every school district in California, and then created a Disney Channel Special on the initiative. The grand prize was won by an inner city school in San Francisco, and the project was praised by California Senators Barbara Boxer and Diane Feinstein, along with, then, Los Angeles Police Chief Willie Williams.

Immediately after the Disney Channel special aired, teachers around the nation begged Disney to bring the competition to THEIR school districts. Unfortunately, the project was scrapped, with Disney citing the expense. At least they did it one time, and The Youth Citizenship Competition was lauded even in the United States Congressional Record May 25th, 1993. California Rep. Bill Baker read, in part: "I would like to congratulate the students of Ann Hankes' eighth grade class at St. Raymond's Middle School in Dublin, CA, who won the American Youth Citizenship Competition in the 10th Congressional District.

"The statewide program, sponsored by the Walt Disney Co., is an academic competition designed to inspire middle school students to take an active role in government by examining a current issue facing their community.

"These young men and women worked diligently on a proposed antismoking ordinance which is one of the toughest issues facing most of our cities today." You can find the entire statement at http://www.fcc.gov/Bureaus/OSEC/library/legislative_histories/1494.pdf.

After I got past his swearing and contempt for women, I worked quite well with Walt.

Hun-ney of a Guy

When Disneyland hired an outside video crew to help with a new production, I got to work closely with the crew's director. He was brilliant, talented, and incredibly difficult to work with for nearly everyone. When he took issue with people, he couldn't agree merely to disagree, he had to humiliate them, squash their dreams, and mangle any last shred of their dignity that struggled to survive his vicious onslaughts. I managed to surf around his spiky energy and stay out of the fray, under the radar. Until, that is, he learned I was a psychic.

"Hey, I'd love to get a reading," he said in a way I understood was more of a command than an inquiry. We arranged a meeting after hours, off property, to do a session.

A quick word here about past lives: even though I frequently see them when I'm doing a reading, as I mentioned before, I'm not convinced we literally hopscotch from body to body through the millennia. I'm much more of the opinion that everything exists simultaneously. We are VERY capable of tapping into another time, and the consciousness of another person, because we're all literally connected, and we're all part of the same soup.

That being said, when I DO receive a strong past-life energy from someone, it always directly parallels a key issue unfolding in his or her current life. It's a way for people to be able to discern the lesson from a safe, detached distance; after all, they're certainly not responsible for something that happened in a past life, before they became the person they are now! See how cool that works?

But, gently refocusing....

During the man's session, I strongly received that he was a merciless warrior on the order of Attila the Hun. I explained that the energy he brought with him from that lifetime made him ruthless and unable to compromise. Instead of agreeing to disagree with his adversaries, he had to relieve them of their heads and smoosh their guts over the burning Gobi Desert sands.

The director immediately "got" it. From the non-threatening vantage point of 1,500 years after the fact, he could acknowledge how the same traits from that untamed time were not as effective in contemporary clashes of will. He truly was able to shift to a kinder, gentler way of dealing with conflict, and became a Hun-ney of a guy. A quick postscript: Shortly after that reading, the man shared something that happened at his sister's home. She and her husband were almost asleep, with their 3-year-old son sleeping between them, when their 5-year-old daughter came into her parents' bedroom. When she saw her brother was there, the girl quietly went back to her own bed.

At breakfast the next morning, the mom asked what that nocturnal visit was all about.

"I had a bad dream that Uncle cut off my brother's head," she said earnestly. "I just wanted to make sure he was OK." Coincidence? I think *not*.

The "Spirited Extras" at Disneyland

As Halloween approached in my first year at Disneyland, I got the bright idea that it would be a cool press release to talk about any "real" ghosts at the Park. Greg usually supported my wild and crazy suggestions, and gave me a green light. I started interviewing the "old timers" at the Park to get the scoop. I got WAY more than I bargained for!

First, I heard the story about an electrician who was working inside Space Mountain one night after the Park had closed. He was standing on the track, adjusting some lights, when someone accidentally switched on the track's power. The worker, the story goes, was immediately electrocuted. Legend has it that guests in the Space Mountain rockets have occasionally heard a man screaming, and have seen disembodied hands appear on their cars. Intrigued, I rounded up some other PR folks and we took a couple of rides. We ALL ended up screaming so loudly we would have drowned out any noisy ghost, but none of us ever saw any hands beyond those we brought on the ride with us.

Next, I spoke with a Park Lead, a supervisor on the Haunted Mansion ride. He made me promise I would never tell his name before he told me several stories. First, frequently, people closing the ride at the end of the night will hear kids laughing. The operators will keep cycling the cars through the ride, looking for the "doom buggy" with the happy munchkins. The children never...ah...materialize.

Then he told me about the time he was closing up, and he saw a man's shoes sticking out from behind one of the long curtains shrouding the exit corridor. "OK, Buddy, ride's closed...time to go," he said as he parted the drapes. There was no one there, and then the shoes disappeared, too.

The third story he shared was the freakiest. Years ago a woman cast member had a younger brother who had a degenerative disease; I think it was Muscular Dystrophy. The boy loved the Park, particularly the Haunted Mansion, and rode it constantly while his sister was on duty. He always sported his favorite red baseball cap. The boy requested that his ashes be scattered around the ride after his death, and his sister reportedly obliged. Frequently now, ride operators closing the attraction for the night will see a boy in a red ball cap showing up in the mirror, but when they turn to talk to him, there's no one there.

As cool as all these stories were, The Powers That Be decided these wouldn't really generate the type of media attention Disneyland wanted. So, I never did get to write that Halloween release. But the next time you're at the Park, tell the kid in the red ball cap, who only shows up in the mirror, that I said, "Hey!"

Tom's a Class Act

A brief tangent: This story really isn't about intuitive ability, but more about honoring everyone, no matter how much earth-time they've logged.

When Tom Hanks, Rob Reiner, and their families came to spend the day at the park, I wasn't escorting them, but I saw the group from a few yards away. This would have been right after *A League of Their Own* and *Sleepless in Seattle*, when Tom became firmly entrenched in "A" List territory.

As I watched, his young son tugged at Tom's shirt to tell him something. This superstar just stopped everything, knelt down on one knee to be at eye level with the boy, and gave the little guy his undivided attention and respect. That, to me, is the definition of being a class act.

House of Destiny!

While I was reveling in my Disney adventures, Paul and I fell deeply, totally, completely in love, got engaged, and eloped to Maui. There was even a glorious double rainbow painted across the sky that morning, and the judge who performed our ceremony cried with us. Everything was just perfect. I never had the feeling of lightness and loving connection with any man like the one I felt with Paul. The other new and wonderful aspect to our deepening relationship was his encouragement for me to come out of the spiritual closet with my psychic abilities. While he wasn't at all into the metaphysical side of life, he respected the fact that I was, and he paid attention to the information I constantly received.

We decided to take the money we *would* have spent on a big wedding and buy a home instead. To collect enough for a healthy down payment, we lived together in his cramped two-bedroom, one-bath cottage for almost a year and kept most of our combined furniture in storage. Several weekends we trooped through open house after open house, searching for that magical "first home" we were so eager to find.

After a few weeks, we contacted a relatively new realtor to help us, and then I had The Dream. It started with me standing in front of a curved brick wall. It seemed odd to me that bricks were laid in more of an arcing shape instead of at 90-degree angles, but heck, it was "only" a dream.

Then it segued to the interior of a little house. I don't remember specific features inside the house, but I DO remember a friendly, playful ghost was showing me around the place. It was as if Casper himself lived nearby and really wanted us to be his new neighbors.

The last part of the dream showed what I took to be the address—"1735." The number was carved on a piece of wood and attached to the front column of the house. I mentally made a note of the three elements, then pretty much forgot about them.

When our realtor met us that Saturday, we were ready for another round of house hunting. He drove us to the lovely little town of Yorba Linda, which, if you're a dyed-in-the-wool Republican, you will recognize as the location of the Richard Nixon Library.

Quick tangent—the popular license plate frame for the upper crust, well-manicured area read, "Yorba Linda. Land of Gracious Living." We were delighted to spot a renegade plate, "Yorba Linda. Land of Pompous Slogans."

But gently refocusing....

The first place we drove up to had an interesting planter box running along the entire front of the house. It was brick, and curved. Hmmmmmm. That was the FIRST confirmation from the dream.

"This is really an historic neighborhood," the realtor said. "In fact, the old Yorba family graveyard is just over that hill right there." HMMMMMMMM. Helloooo, friendly neighborhood Casper! Confirmation number two.

Paul and I toured the cute little place and did the potential new house equivalent of kicking the tires—opening and shutting drawers and cabinets, flushing toilets, turning on the sprinklers. It all looked great, and we loved it.

"What would the monthly payments be?" Paul asked.

The realtor scribbled on his clipboard, punched some numbers in his calculator, and scribbled some more.

"With taxes and escrow, $1,735."

"We'll take it!" I said. Paul looked at me quizzically. "Honey," I started to explain earnestly, "I had this dream…."

Paul put his hand on my arm to silence me.

"Yep, we'll take it," he said, rolling his eyes only slightly. He knew better than to argue with my dreams! And in that sweet predestined home we lived happily ever after—for a while.

Enter the Dead People

During one of my first visits with Paul to Seattle to visit his brother and two sisters, we all ended up visiting Pike Place Market. For the uninitiated, this marvelous melting pot of ancient and contemporary, kitsch and treasure is one of the oldest continuously operating public markets in the nation. It's kind of like a daily street fair, with live entertainment, crafts, every imaginable kind of food, photographs—you name it—I promise you it's *somewhere* in that glorious, rambling circus of a Farmer's Market.

Pam, who had first introduced me to her brother Paul at Disneyland, suggested the two of us split off from the rest of the group to explore. Like two rambunctious kids, we raced through the throngs, applauded the fish-catchers, tasted the cheese samples, sniffed the various vats of coffee beans, and marveled at all the different kinds of apples. Our attention-deficit tour eventually led us to a little corner apothecary shop, fragrant with the scent of dried herbs and flavored tobaccos.

"Oooooh, look!" I said delightedly, pointing to a "The Tarot Reader is IN" sign. "We GOTTA do that!" Pam sighed with resignation as I steered her into the little shop. A beautiful young woman with striking red hair was shuffling a deck of cards.

I looked at Pam with pleading eyes. She groaned, but scooted in next to me as I sat down at the table across from the woman.

The tarot reader looked up from the cards, and regarded me quizzically.

"Do I know you?" she asked.

"Here we go!" Pam muttered good-naturedly.

I elbowed Pam and smiled at the woman.

"Not from this life," I answered cheerfully. "But I'm certain we've met in others."

"I'm Sita," she said, smiling. She offered me the deck. I shuffled it and handed it back. Sita started laying out cards, and then stopped, staring intently at the tableau unfolding before her. She looked up at me again, and narrowed her eyes.

"You're psychic," she said. "*Very* psychic."

"Ya *think?*" Pam asked. I shushed her.

"In fact," Sita continued, "You have a very strong ability to talk to the dead."

I started shaking my head. "Ah, no. THAT I don't do," I answered.

"But you DO," she insisted, and set down the deck of cards to stare at me. "In fact, I want you to connect with my daughter who died when she was three. Tell me what you see."

"I don't SEE anything," I started to protest—and that's when it happened. Clear as day, I suddenly saw, in my mind's eye, a beautiful little girl with long strawberry blonde curls, dressed in an emerald green velvet dress, peering out from behind an imposing old man. The man wasn't stooped, but wore his decades like a royal robe. He had a leather pouch over his shoulder and knee-high leather boots. There was something about dried grass and flowers.

His slightly confrontational posture showed me he was protective of the child but quite curious about me, and it appeared they were standing in a flowering meadow in another country. England. It was England. And the man was a minister, but also...other things. The child's name was Alexandra. I conveyed all this to Sita, and she gasped.

"That's what we were going to name her, but we named her Faye instead," Sita said softly. "That man is my great-grandfather, Sabine Baring-Gould. They're at the family estate in Devon. He was a minister and an herbalist, which is why you see the meadow and the leather pouch with the dried grasses and flowers. And," she paused, her eyes drilling into mine, "He composed the hymn, 'Onward, Christian Soldiers.'"

Pam, Sita, and I shared the stunned silence.

"I...I guess maybe I CAN do this," I finally said. But there was MORE proof. As we sat there and I continued to focus on the little girl, she morphed into being several years older, and told me what was happening to Sita at that point in time. Over and over again, as the beautiful child grew up before my eyes and shared what was unfolding at each state of her and Sita's life, Sita confirmed the information. I was amazed at the detail I was shown, and Sita was SO comforted to know her lovely, beloved daughter had never really left her side.

That day Sita gave me the gift of knowing I didn't just see dead family members of MINE, I could also let other people know what was going on with their own friends and family in the spirit world. To this day, she remains a mentor and dear friend. There is just no way I can ever thank her for her patience, encouragement, and love! She opened my eyes, and my world. Since her patient insistence that I could clearly see into the spirit dimension, I have had the great honor of helping thousands of grieving people reconnect with loved ones on the other side. It never fails to thrill, awe, and humble me to see how the worlds of the living and the dead intertwine in sacred symmetry.

Grim Glimpse

Being highly intuitive isn't always fun. One evening Paul and I were watching TV in our Anaheim home when a story came on the air about a woman who claimed a black man had carjacked her, and her two children were in the vehicle at the time.

"Oh my GOD," I said to Paul. "She killed her two kids! Her car is in the lake!" Paul looked at me then looked back at the TV. The woman was sobbing, dramatically devastated that her children were missing because of this horrible man.

Of course this was the chilling Susan Smith story from South Carolina, and the woman had indeed fabricated the account of a man forcing her from her car while her children were whisked away. She had killed them in cold blood and their tiny bodies were eventually found, still in the submerged car. You heard it here first.

Perhaps the toughest thing about getting information intuitively like that is the sense of helplessness; you want to say something to the police, but accepting tips from psychics is not exactly normal law enforcement procedure. Yet. We're working on it!

Boat of Sorrow

Traipsing around the time-space continuum in my own out-of-order order definitely isn't all fun and games. And so it was in spring of 1995, when I had a rather disturbing "dream." It wasn't a complete vision, but more of a snapshot.

In my dream, it appeared as if a huge ship had somehow beached itself in a dried up lakebed. The entire side of the ship was gone, and white birds fluttered around the exposed levels of the ship as it sat in the scooped out space where the water had been. There was just such a sense of desolation and ominous silence about this scene, and it troubled me deeply.

A few days later as I was reading the newspaper, I gasped. There was the exact image I'd seen, and it was an AP photograph of the devastation from the Oklahoma City bombing. What I assumed was a dried up lake bed was actually debris caused by the blast, the "boat without one side" was the ripped open Federal Building, and the birds were actually thousands of pieces of paper, eerily hanging in the air in the heart-wrenching photo.

I bowed my head and prayed for safe passage for the 168 people who so cruelly and abruptly had been ushered to the other side of the veil. Meanwhile, back on the home front, another big shift was on the horizon.

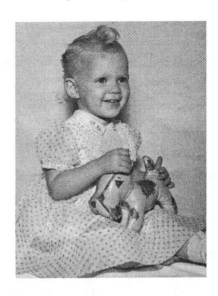

Above: This was half a century ago, but I still clearly remember the little flowers on my dress were purple. **Below:** Jeffrey, David, Donald, and I check out the Christmas ham.

Above: I didn't just play with cats—here I am with a piglet on a cousin's farm near State College, Pa.; and with Raincloud, one of my hamsters. **Below:** Jeff and I pose with Alibaba in front of the lamb house Dad built. I named the critter, of course.

Above: The Bartges kids and Sandy Claws smile for a Christmas card photo. **Below:** Posing with our camper-bus during a vacation road trip.

Above: That's me in a National Guard chopper flying across Pennsylvania to cover the 1977 Johnstown Flood for The Morning Call.

Above: The United Research Light Center under construction in Black Mountain, North Carolina. Founder Jim Goure recruited me in 1979 to be the resident psychic and newsletter editor.

Above: Even when I was the Advertising & Promotions Manager at a Miami TV station in the 80's, I was already feeling the "Mickey Mouse" vibes in my future.

Above left: I was rocking the Lady Di look in the '80s before *she* did. **Right:** All my bratty friends called this my "Other than that, Mrs. Lincoln, how was the play?" look.

Right: After my brain aneurysm, my hair grew back pretty quickly—at right is a picture about three weeks after my near-death experience in 1989. **Below:** My Miami friend Kathy Echroll brought Tina Turner wigs with her when she visited me in Wichita while I was recuperating.

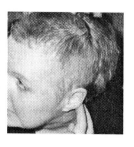

Left: Disneyland Main Street Conductor Paul Lankford swept me off my feet when I started working at the Happiest Place on Earth in 1991. We both realized on our first date we were going to end up married.

Above: Belle, Beast and I pose for a photo at the 1994 Radio and Television News Directors Association conference at the Los Angeles Convention Center. **Below:** Disneyland PR Manager Greg Albrecht, one of my favorite bosses of all time.

Above: The New Zealand "studio" set for the Legoland California pre-launch promotional campaign shoot. **Left:** Sister-in-law Pam Espinosa, Paul and I act relatively silly in front of the Albert Einstein model made entirely of regulation Lego bricks as the Carlsbad Legoland park slowly takes shape in 1999.

Above: Paul and I make our pilgrimage to Walt Disney World in 2000—one of the big things on Paul's bucket list. **Below:** We lift off on our first and only hot air balloon ride.

Left: We make it to Sedona in November 2000, and Paul gets the gift of three more months of life.

Below: Paul insists we take one last picture on the balcony of his San Diego Hospice room February 9, 2001. His grace and calm determination to leave with dignity, and on his terms, helped all of us deal with his death three days later.

Above: Sea World General Curator Jim Antrim takes us out to scatter Paul's ashes off the coast of San Diego. **Below:** A faint but distinctive angelic image showed up on Jeffrey's picture of one of the three pelicans who surrounded us for Paul's ceremony.

Above: One of my Practical Spirituality 101 classes in Asheville, N.C. I warn students they're not getting out of the room until they can do an accurate reading—and it always works. **Below:** Timber, a magnificent 16-year-old gray wolf dog, calmly receives a Reiki treatment from me.

Chapter 9
Of Dolphins and Danes

After logging five years with Disney, Sea World made me an offer I couldn't refuse to be its director of public relations at the San Diego Park. Before I accepted, though, Paul and I did an "undercover" trip to check out the vibes.

I had to feel for myself if the employees were happy. I had to see what kind of environmental standards the park had. Moreover, most importantly, I had to see if the animals were treated with dignity and respect.

I psyched it out, and it felt wonderful to me. I also felt an instant connection to the man who would be my new boss, Bill Thomas, and the men with whom I would be working closely—general curator Jim Antrim, and head veterinarian Dr. Jim McBain. All three had integrity, were brilliant, and showed a great sense of humor.

The other confirmation I needed came a night after I did a round of interviews with the guys. As always, I prayed before I fell asleep, and asked for some kind of divine sign if Sea World was where I was supposed to go. To my delight, in my dreams that evening, I was flying over the park, and all the whales and dolphins were talking to me. Let me be clear—there was no plane involved. It was just ME, arms out, hair blowing in the wind, gliding over the pools and joyfully connecting with the animals. I gave Sea World my "yes" the next morning.

Just a few weeks after I took over the reins of the Public Relations department, an event happened that would change all the textbooks on marine mammals. We got a call that an infant gray whale had beached near Marina del Rey, just 20 miles southwest of Los Angeles, and rescuers managed to load the 13-foot, 8-inch-long, 1,673-pound "baby girl" into a truck. With teams of volunteers pouring seawater over her and a police escort to speed the trip, the rescuers raced against time to get the calf to Sea World. It was her only chance of survival, and a slim chance at that.

The whale was covered with cuts from Pacific waves throwing her against the rocks and rolling her over and over on the beach. Her umbilical cord was still attached, and there was no way of knowing if she had nursed and received the critically important colostrum from her mother's first milk.

She was miraculously still alive after the two-hour dash down California's Interstate 5, and the Sea World Animal Care Specialists gingerly lifted the calf out of the truck with a sling and a crane. They lowered her into a medical pool in the park's back-stage Animal Care Complex. Six Sea World team members in wet suits were waiting in the pool to receive her, and supported her, three on each side, while they walked her in a big circle around the pool. Otherwise, the weak, injured calf would have sunk to the bottom of the pool and immediately drowned.

Because I had just started working at Sea World, no one there knew I actively used my intuitive abilities as much as possible. That night, I knelt by the edge of the med pool and thought at the struggling gray whale, "How can we help you live?"

Immediately I was hit between the eyes with the words, "Amino acids!"

Since I'd never taken a biology class in college, I had NO idea what that meant. Undeterred, I assumed a casual attitude, walked up to Dr. Tom Reidarson, a staff veterinarian, and off-handedly asked, "Have you checked her amino acid levels yet?"

Dr. Reidarson ordered the tests, and when the results came back, the calf's taurine levels were critically low. Taurine, I learned, regulates both the heart and the brain. The Animal

Care team immediately began administering massive amounts of natural taurine along with the protein-rich formula they created for her, and the calf made an astonishingly rapid shift from "surviving" to "thriving."

When I would come to visit her, I'd put my hands against the thick glass of the viewing window, and J.J., as she was eventually named, would immediately swim over to me. She'd slowly glide back and forth in front of the glass, regarding me with one huge, soulful eye at a time. I would send her love and appreciation; she would send me murky images of where she started her life.

During the time Sea World's incredible team of veterinarians and Animal Care Specialists were rehabilitating J.J. and preparing her for life in the wild, researchers were gaining valuable information about gray whale growth, respiration, heart rate, and other facts that had never been known. J.J. provided an unprecedented opportunity to learn volumes about this magnificent, illusive species.

Meanwhile, I was making J.J. an international story with regular press conferences, and spectacular, never-before-seen gray whale video and photos from our talented photographers. The media blitz culminated in a live CNN broadcast of her release back into the ocean a year later, and a National Geographic special. I arranged to have J.J.'s release shown live on the Shamu Stadium Jumbotron screen to students and Sea World visitors. It was a powerful, historical moment for all of us. Less than three days back in the wild, J.J. managed to lose her tracking device, and there was no further contact. Still, she swam into the history books with the invaluable, unprecedented view of the gray whale she shared with us all.

I was so thankful to have had the opportunity to connect with this sensitive, brilliant being on loan to humans for such a short time.

Whoooooo Knew?

Paul and I were kind of a mixed marriage—he loved wilderness hiking and camping in Yosemite—and I loved room service.

Our compromise was to rent an RV to go camping, combining the great outdoors with flush toilets and showers. During a mini-camping trip to Big Bear, California, a beautiful mountain town a few hours outside of Anaheim, we discovered a fantastic wild animal preserve. Wolves, birds of prey, bears, bobcats—any animal that's been hurt—is brought there for rehabilitation and, if they recover sufficiently, eventual release back into the woods. Some have been hit by cars; others injured by getting entangled in man-made obstacles like power wires, and still others victims of stupid or deliberately cruel human actions.

While the public can view the animals, it's definitely not a "zoo." The caring staff leads groups through the maze of enclosures with stern instructions on how to keep similar injuries from ever happening to other wild animals. Visitors receive a newfound respect for these magnificent creatures who were here first, and who deserve our respect and compassion.

Paul and I were particularly enthralled with the wolf pack. When the faint shriek of a distant siren split the calm at the preserve, the wolves stopped in their tracks and pointed their chins skyward to echo the mournful tone. It was simultaneously beautiful and bone chilling.

A short walk from the wolf pen was a huge Great Horned Owl. His shattered wing, the result of a bullet, would never allow him the freedom of release.

The stoic bird perched right at eye level, in the branch of a tree that was surrounded with a swath of chicken wire. We calmly regarded each other, his amber eyes boring into my teal ones.

"I'm so sorry you're in that cage," I thought at him.

"Who among you is not?" he retorted. I gasped and stepped back, astounded at the deep wisdom and soul truth of his reply.

How quick we are to assume animals function primarily on base instinct alone, seeking only to eat, reproduce, and survive.

How much richer our lives will be when we're constantly communicating with them on the deep spiritual level to which they are tuned!

Anniversary Dinner

I was blissfully happy with Paul in a way I had never even dared imagine. There was no posturing, no agenda, and no controlling or manipulative energy in our marriage. Instead, there was tenderness, consideration, respect, *great* sex, and so much laughter. For our fifth anniversary, he and I planned a weeklong bed and breakfast tour of Sonoma, gradually working our way over to Yosemite for the final two nights. The park had a special meaning for Paul. He'd found great peace there before he and I had met when he was healing his heart after his father died in 1989—the same year I experienced my *own* death.

Our week was perfect, packed with wine tasting, hikes through the forest, spectacular sunsets and lots of togetherness. We stayed at a hotel right outside of the park, and the chances of us getting in to the popular Ahwahnee Lodge for dinner on our actual anniversary night were slim to none. "I think we need a backup plan," Paul said as we surveyed the throng of people with reservations waiting to be seated.

"Nope. I know it's OK!" I said confidently. I "thought" at the hostess, and in moments we were being whisked away to a prime location in front of a huge window. Paul was thrilled, and said, "There's only one thing missing. We haven't seen any deer yet."

Within 30 seconds, THREE deer slowly ambled into frame, coming up to the shrub right in front of our window to nibble leaves. Paul just laughed.

Our waiter was a clean-cut young man with blond hair pulled back in a ponytail, and gold wire-rimmed glasses. Although I was focusing on Paul and the great time we were enjoying together, I kept getting an urgent intuitive message for our waiter. Normally I do NOT read strangers, but the information was refusing to leave my brain, and demanded that

I share it. When the waiter returned to our table with rolls and butter, I took a deep breath and said, "You know, if you'd go back to school, you'd become an incredibly successful architect."

Without skipping a beat, the waiter looked up and said, "But I dropped out because the math was too hard!"

One of the things I just loved about Paul was how he didn't really understand how I did my psychic work, but he respected it and encouraged me. As the waiter and I continued our rather spirited exchange, Paul just smiled and buttered his roll.

"You could get on TOP of the math," I answered. "You just have such a bright future in design and architecture if you pursue it."

"Hey, thanks!" the guy said enthusiastically. I strongly feel he DID go back to school. If anyone knows a successful blond architect who waited tables in Yosemite in the fall of 1997, I'd love to hear from you!

Plane Obstinate

One of the funkier aspects of being tuned to a highly sensitive level is that you see, feel, and hear things that might get lost in the shuffle for other people. For instance, when someone lies, the colors around that person become dense and murky. When people are angry, sparks shoot off them and pierce the energy fields of those around them. And, when someone just doesn't like you, there's a suffocating gray smog that oozes from him or her and tries to glom on to you, dimming your light, dragging you down and rendering you immobile.

During business meetings, particularly, it can be challenging. When a supervisor or colleague is saying one thing, you can feel, and sometimes even see, how he or she is thinking something radically different.

Of course, that spiffy all-purpose affirmation in the front of this book can keep any and all of that negative gook from having any power over you when you use it. Just reading or silently reciting the words automatically raises your energetic level to a higher vibration, and anything that connects with you must be of that positive vibration or higher.

After two fascinating years at Sea World, I was given an offer I couldn't refuse from The Lego Company. The Danish-based toy giant was planning on opening its third Lego theme park for kids, and it decided on a prime location in Southern California between Disneyland and Sea World. They wanted me to head up the Public Relations department and coordinate the huge international press event for the opening of Legoland California the following year. Paul was thrilled for me, and encouraged me to follow my heart.

Keeping the powerful affirmation in my mind was essential in the pressure-cooker atmosphere of Legoland. I constantly kept my radar active during the long, demanding workweek. One co-worker in particular was always tense and rather angry with everyone. I just beamed positive white light in her direction and focused on leading my team.

She was thrilled when she closed the deal for a partnership with a commuter airline that flew in and out of a tiny airport adjacent to Legoland, and wanted me to write a press release and drum up media attention.

"Thanks for letting me know," I told her. "I'll work on it." Actually, I got a HUGE red light, my instant internal signal not to do anything with the information. There were no specifics as to why, but there was no mistaking the message that it would be a bad idea—*seriously* bad—to move forward with any proactive marketing to trumpet the new partnership between the kids' park and this small airline.

Daily the woman asked to see a press release, and daily I dodged her for two weeks. Then, it all became clear.

Without warning, the commuter airline went out of business.

Had I created a big splash about the partnership, the instant demise of the airline would have been a very negative reflection on the park. How could they trust us with their children if we were in cahoots with a company of questionable reliability? It would have been a PR nightmare.

The woman, of course, never mentioned it again. Meanwhile, I breathed a silent prayer of thanks for the intuitive intervention. This was yet another proof of why it's important to trust those strong "hunches," especially when there's no real logical reason to do so.

Magical New Zealand

From its rolling grassy hills dotted with sheep, to towering cliffs, dense forests, ferny bowers, and rich Maori culture, New Zealand immediately catapulted into my heart when it became my temporary home for three glorious weeks in the summer of 1998. The island nation that had never even been on my radar before moved into focus when the Los Angeles advertising agency creating the series of promotional spots for the launch of Legoland decided to move the production there rather than pay Screen Actors Guild (SAG) fees for a state-side shoot.

Legoland's marketing director couldn't make the trip, so as Legoland's communications director, I got to dust off my passport, retrieve my luggage from under the bed, and spend 17 hours in a plane heading to the land of kiwis, rainforests, glaciers, and volcanoes. Paul was holding down the fort at home.

While I was waiting for my flight and browsing through an LAX airport gift shop, "the voices" told me to buy a flashlight. I thought it odd, but picked out a red one, paid for it, and stashed it in my purse on the way to my departure gate. This was pre-9/11, when we could still take such things on a plane without being challenged.

During the flight, I was sitting next to the agency's art director—let's call him Joe. He was a brilliant, creative, and funny guy—which made for a great marathon conversation. We enjoyed a kind of instant trust and familiarity with that many hours side by side, and one of the topics that came up was the fact that everyone has natural intuitive ability. Joe was intrigued that I tapped into mine on a regular basis.

The first few days after our arrival on the North Island some of us had a chance to explore Auckland and the surrounding countryside while the final details for our shoot were being locked down. We watched urban climbers rappelling off the sides of skyscrapers. We tasted diabolical libations called "Lemon Ruskies" in a funky little bar perched high over the city. We sampled local cuisine ranging from hand-held meat pies to melt-in-your-mouth fish dishes to exquisite local wines.

It was a side trip to a Maori center, though, which made me want to stay in New Zealand forever. The music, the dancing, the chanting and singing—it was all so strangely familiar and comforting. And, I was smitten with the Maori people! Before the missionaries arrived to pray and prey, the Maori believed a sacred life force permeated everything, connecting all of creation. Reincarnation, telepathy, energy healing, honoring all life—it's all woven into the fabric of their culture. I saw and felt it shining through their eyes and smiles. They recognized me, too. I eagerly soaked in the fantastic vibes.

When we received word that our studio was finally ready for us to start filming, we reluctantly tore ourselves away from exploring this magnificent country and got down to work.

After driving several hours deep into the countryside, we discovered our "studio" was a huge storehouse for onions that had not yet, thankfully, been used for that pungent purpose. Inside the metal building, a stage had been constructed for our shoot, and an army of lights encircled the platform. Local children were recruited to play the parts of youngsters discovering mystical clues heralding the coming of this park built around the idea of building.

"So if you're so psychic," Joe asked me the morning of the first day of our shoot, "how's it going to go today?"

I quickly went to level and saw the answer. "We'll start out well," I said, "and then run into some technical issues that will shut us down briefly. We'll get those fixed, and then have trouble with lights. But that will also be resolved, and things will go great."

"We'll see!" Joe laughed.

One of the key special effects throughout the campaign was a thick fog, which added to the anticipation and mystery the commercials were creating. A few hours into the shoot, the fog machine conked out.

Joe looked at me quizzically. "This is probably that technical issue," I told him. "They'll get it back up before too long." He slowly shook his head, hesitant to believe me completely.

About an hour later, the fog machine was back on line.

Another hour into the shoot, though, one of the children's little flashlights broke.

"Where the heck are we going to get another torch way out here in the middle of nowhere?" the director yelled. "We're gonna be down for HOURS!"

I reached into my purse and pulled out the Lego-red flashlight I'd bought at the airport.

"Will this one work?" I asked.

Everyone turned and looked at me.

"Don't ask," Joe said to the group. The shoot stayed right on schedule. And, as was my lifelong pattern of downplaying intuitive hits, we just didn't mention it again.

Ocean Trees

Decades ago, I had a vivid dream that would periodically replay in my night flights. I walked down a slight incline that was covered with pebbles and larger stones, worn smooth by the ocean's persistent waves. A road starting from the rocky beach and leading out into the ocean would appear, then disappear, then appear again. Trees lined the mystical pathway.

One of the huge perks of being lured away from Sea World to join the executive opening team at Legoland was getting to travel for the Danish-based Lego Company—a lot! I got to have that fantastic adventure in New Zealand, and traveled several times to Denmark, Germany, England, and Poland.

During a three-week working trip to the Lego Company's headquarters in Billund, Denmark, a Danish colleague frequently invited me to join her and her two children, seven and 10, for weekend excursions. We joked that the blond, blue-eyed children looked more like me than her, so I became their "Mor" the days we explored together.

We visited the oldest Viking village in Jutland; we toured the "Fiskehaven," a Danish version of Sea World; we climbed the rickety winding stairs in an ancient church; we posed next to huge white statues staring out over the North Sea. Discovering these spots was magical, and somehow quite familiar.

During one particular outing, as Karen turned the car onto a road parallel to the ocean, I started to get a wave of chills running up my spine. She parked the car on a bluff, and the kids tumbled out and started running for the water.

Slowly, I stepped out of the little vehicle and stared, trying to take in everything at once. We were on the same rocky incline I'd seen so many times before in my dreams. And, as in my dreams, there was a row of trees rising from the ocean waves, leading out to an unseen point. Wave upon wave of chills flooded down my back.

"Ah…Karen?" I said quietly. "What IS this place?"

"There's a road here that is only visible at low tide," she said. "It takes you out to an island you can't see from here. It's a very ancient place." The chills come back as I write this, years after the fact.

There's incredible wisdom and truth in our dreams, whether it's literal or symbolic. In that state beyond the limitations of the conscious mind, we're free to traipse back and forth in time, and to connect with everyone, and everything, on a cosmic, spiritual level. Embrace the possibilities!

Chapter 10
Lengthening Shadows

Any time you start to forget there's a divine thread connecting everything and everyone, you'll get a gentle reminder to release your attachment to the outcome, and just TRUST the universe. The real challenge is in training yourself to notice these opportunities, and then to learn and grow from them. Find the lesson and you'll find the gift, no matter how tough the situation looks on the surface.

In November of '98, Paul went in for routine outpatient surgery on the cartilage in his knee. The day before the procedure, his preliminary blood work revealed he had adult onset diabetes. That was the first big negative thing that happened to us. Then about two weeks after his surgery, we noticed a BB-sized lump on his lip. This is where my subconscious awareness that had been pushed under the surface for so many years popped up, and I told Paul's doctor I thought it might be cancer. The doctor brushed me off and said, "No, he just bit his lip during the knee surgery. It's a little blood blister. It will go away." It did *not*.

Over the next few weeks and months, Paul's "blood blister" kept growing. The doctor insisted it was just "calcifying," and it would soon disappear. I asked again, "Could it be cancer?" The doctor said that was just ridiculous. At the point where the "blood blister" was about the size of a peanut M&M—forgive me, I don't know medical metric measurements—the doctor decided to remove it through an outpatient procedure. It was two weeks before the huge international opening of Legoland, scheduled for March 20, 1999. I knew what the diagnosis was going to be as I just sat in the family room at the hospital, praying, as the hours dragged on and on.

The waiting room emptied out. I asked the nurse at the reception desk to please check on Paul's progress. She returned to the desk and couldn't make eye contact with me, simply saying, "It's taking a bit longer than the doctor anticipated."

Finally, the doctor came into the waiting room to deliver his preliminary diagnosis. He said Paul's "cyst" was spiral cell cancer, and they had removed half of Paul's lower lip. When I rushed back into the recovery room to be with him, Paul was lying there alone. All the other patients had already been discharged.

As I walked up to his side, his tear-filled eyes locked on mine. I gently took his hand, and in a raspy voice he choked, "So they said it's cancer." The doctor told him this while he was lying there, alone. It was such an insensitive and cruel thing to do—especially because I was just a few feet away in the waiting room.

We immediately took action. We changed Paul's doctors, and he was assigned an oncologist. He had another surgery to excise clear margins, and this is when we discovered that Paul had an allergy to morphine—a development that was going to become more critical as the disease progressed. The diagnosis was changed from spiral cell cancer to malignant melanoma, and we learned the prognosis was six months.

Divine Decisions

One of our greatest divine gifts, and ironically one of our biggest challenges, is free will. We always get to decide what we bring into our lives. I believe we choose our parents, our siblings, and in a general sense, the major lessons that we desire to learn in a particular lifetime, even before the sperm meets the egg that will eventually become us.

In the delightful melee of coincidences, dimensions, colors, sounds, concepts and fleeting glimpses that weave together reality, I believe before we incarnate we have something of an organizational meeting with our spiritual "task forces."

We get to choose the major life lessons we desire to learn in the upcoming incarnation, and whom in our spiritual posse we want to bring with us to help us learn those lessons. We get to choose the things that we are going to attract to us, and the meaning we are going to give to those things. Triumph or tragedy? Despair or epiphany? Love or hate? *We* get to decide.

And of course, we get to choose when…and how…we exit. Although we create an outline of all these major milestones that will unfold over the coming days, months, years and/or decades, the one constant for us all is that "Free Will" thing. According to the "fine print" in that cosmic "See Earth in the New Millennium" brochure that caught our (third) eye, at any time we can yell the spiritual equivalent of "REWRITE," and change our script at will.

I had always believed all of this in theory, but that day in June of 1989, the day of the aneurysm, that day where I hovered between this world and the next, I received the cosmic gift of actually becoming "the living proof." The key word, here, is "living."

Still, even with my very personal knowing of that sacred, divine order that governs and protects us, there was just no way I could calmly and with gentle detachment immediately accept that this horrible, humiliating, debilitating exit strategy Paul faced was something he either consciously or subconsciously choose. It just hurt too much even to consider. Wisdom, though, can be slow to show itself….

One Foot In Front Of the Other….

I had to be Paul's strong emotional support. I had to become his medical advocate. I had to keep a clear head. And, I had to oversee an international event that included 350 journalists from literally around the world, live remote broadcasts to numerous nations, an entire media village and thousands of little details just waiting to topple one another like so many demonic dominos.

Thanks to my incredible PR team and the support of the other departments at the Park, Legoland's opening was flawless. We ended up getting over one billion documented media impressions through the end of that year. If you're not a media geek, that means people saw on TV, heard on the radio or read in print media something about the Park one *billion* times. We also won the International Association of Amusement Parks and Attractions Brass Ring for having the best Web site for Parks in our attendance category. That rocked. But, it couldn't begin to cancel out the soul pain of Paul's death sentence.

If I had not developed my unwavering link to God that's at the core of everything in my life, there is no way I would have survived this heartbreaking turn of events. After a lifetime of being hurt by the men in my life, I had finally found what real love was all about. I felt such joy just looking into Paul's eyes, and frequently awoke in the middle of the night to discover we'd been holding hands in our sleep. There was such peace and comfort in his arms; I felt so safe and so loved. I could not bear the thought of losing him, and I could not bear the thought of the physical, mental, and emotional anguish he was already starting to endure.

As I prayed through my sobs to understand what karmic dance we were doing, the answer came to me quite clearly. As Paul had taught me to live in joyful love, with an open heart, I was going to help him die with the same grace and trust. I had danced with death myself; I knew I could help him release any fear, and live what days we had left together with joy and gratitude for every minute. I knew this brave man would never even consider taking on the victim role.

Thinking about how I was supposed to fulfill my destiny of raising world consciousness would have to wait. My heart was being called to a higher purpose much closer to home.

Paul immediately completed an advance directive. His father Gene had died from skin cancer that progressed into lung cancer. Paul saw how his father had died piece by piece, getting carved up in futile operation after operation. It was a horrible situation, exacerbated by the fact Gene had heart failure, paramedics were summoned, and he spent an agonizing several more weeks alive, despite his wishes just to die gently. Paul did not want to have that experience.

We also realized that even though we could not control the disease, we could control our reaction to it. We started fighting fear with facts, and we spent hours on the Internet. We went to the John Wayne Cancer Institute in Southern California. We talked to other specialists, and we also made a pact that when we got to the final time, we would visit Disney World. Paul had worked at Disneyland for nearly 30 years but had never seen the other Park.

We also created a list of the top 20 things we wanted to do—Paul's own version of a "bucket list" long before the popular 2007 movie. This turned out to be a very powerful spiritual tool, helping Paul sort through all the peripheral things and concentrate on what really mattered. What was truly important to him for his quality of life, and his spiritual ease? The list went the whole gamut—from Paul waiting to live to see the new Star Wars movie, *Phantom Menace*, to being alive for my June birthday and his sister's July wedding. These very specific goals gave a strong focus and purpose to his life.

On the Roller Coaster

This is where we got on the medical roller coaster so familiar to all patients and families in similar situations. Of course, Paul required additional surgeries. Both Paul and I had a bizarre sense of humor. After he had an ear-to-ear neck dissection to check some lymph nodes, I called him "my Pez dispenser," which always made him laugh. He also started doing chemo, hoping to buy time to make it to his sister's wedding several months away.

Paul was given such a lethal dose of the chemical cocktail that he was admitted to the hospital for the entire week of the procedure. Besides being psychic, I'm a certified hypnotherapist, and I hypnotized him daily. I gave him the suggestion that his body would take what it needed from the chemicals, and gently eliminate the rest.

While he was actually hooked up to the chemo IV, we walked up and down the hospital corridors, talking and laughing, as he pushed the pole in front of him. When we got back to his room, doctors and nurses would come in and say "Don't you feel like you have the flu? Don't you want to throw up?" He would answer, "I feel like I want a hamburger!"

Instead of the medical team wondering why he was having such a different experience, and finding out if there was something here that might help their other patients, it was the elephant-in-the-living room scenario. The attitude seemed to be, "We don't know about this, we don't understand this, we haven't learned about this, so we're going to pretend it's just not happening." Imagine what a difference holistic medicine could make to relieve pain and suffering!

Besides his ability to take the chemo regimen in stride, another amazing thing was Paul's reaction to the whole situation. When he started radiation treatments, his attitude was, "We're going to do what we can." There was a 19-year-old boy also getting radiation. Patients got to know one another while they were waiting for their sessions. Paul told me he felt so sorry for this boy, because he had never had a chance to live. Paul said that he had had a really good life—and he was only 46. His attitude was phenomenal the entire time.

The attitude of the doctor makes all the difference in the world, too. The oncologist, when we would go in to see him, would cross his arms across his chest, not make eye contact with us, and ask, "How's the tumor?" Meanwhile, the plastic surgeon who had worked on Paul was wonderful. He would come out into the waiting room, sit down next to Paul, put his arm around him and say, "Hey, Buddy, how's your life going?"

What a difference! And what a different emotional experience it was for Paul visiting the doctor who showed his caring!

The oncologist treated Paul as though he were an embarrassing failure, and that was painfully obvious.

In addition to the medical roller coaster, we were on an intense personal roller coaster, too. Initially Paul wasn't going to tell his friends at Disneyland. He didn't want to worry these people and burden them with his personal challenges.

But as he and I spoke—I was functioning as his spiritual counselor, his wife and his best friend—I reminded him these people were his second family. He had grown up with these friends, and they had been a vital part of his life for 10, 20 even 30 years. He needed their support, and they needed to know what was going on. He couldn't deprive them of the opportunity to know about his situation, and to use in the most sacred way possible whatever precious time they had left together.

So, he took them into his confidence. He brought death out of the closet at Disneyland, honestly answering questions, and starting a whole skin cancer awareness crusade at the Park. He got people to get their skin checked by their doctors, and dozens of them had precancerous growths removed. Who knows how many lives Paul saved in just the first few months after his diagnosis!

Everyone started using huge pump jars of sun block before they ventured out into the Park, and they'd slather up religiously. Paul totally raised consciousness. He was also deluged with cards, letters, and phone calls from his friends. I decided to have a "Get Well, Dammit!" party at our home in San Diego. A bunch of Paul's friends from Anaheim came down for the day.

With all this positive attention he was getting from his friends, and the open discussions he and I were having, Paul rallied, and was able to go back to work. Instead of thinking, "How could this possibly happen to me," he wanted to make his life count for something. He took on the mammoth task of lobbying Disney to change the dress code policy to allow any employee to wear a hat with a wide, protective brim.

Since the Park opened in 1955, the strict existing wardrobe policy required Cast Members to wear only hats that themed with their costumes. Paul said that wasn't right, and took on the Disney establishment.

When Paul applied to increase his life insurance policy to help me after he crossed over, he found out he had to be alive by January 1 of the following year for the increase to take effect. As part of his hilarious/disgusting sense of humor, he said to his friends at Disneyland, "Have you guys seen the movie *Weekend at Bernie's*? If I don't make it to the first of the year, I want you to tie me to the back of the tram and put a rope around my arm so I can still direct traffic, and they'll never know."

By infusing humor into a situation that was so tragically serious, Paul got all his friends openly communicating. People were being more realistic about life, death, and what really mattered.

Spirit Doctors Without Borders

While Paul navigated his terminal illness with grace and dignity, I considered it an honor, and a sacred responsibility, to share this journey with him.

Despite the fact that on a spiritual level I knew this sacred dance was part of a greater plan, on emotional and mental levels, the sorrow I felt was devastating. I constantly prayed to understand the reason for Paul's suffering and impending death. I prayed to overcome my own ego, which sometimes couldn't cope with the thought of losing him. I prayed to make every moment we shared special, honoring the time we still shared together. These prayers, I prayed constantly.

In addition to my own spiritual healing work, I leaned heavily on my brilliant, compassionate acupuncturist, Erin Raskin, MS, L.Ac., of San Diego. During one particular session, she carefully placed the needles, put the lavender pillow over my eyes and gently shut the treatment room door behind her as she left me to "cook" on the table. Immediately after the door closed, I heard a voice from the ceiling urgently announce, "Kali!"

I was suddenly aware of the presence of a *very* strong female energy standing by my right side. I could feel her working in my energy field, yanking things out, healing blockages and sealing me back up. It definitely wasn't a gentle, "Ohhh, you poor thing! Let me make you feel better" kind of energy. It was more of a "We WILL heal this RIGHT NOW and you will get BACK in the FIGHT!" I was honored, overwhelmed and completely baffled.

When Erin came back in a while later, I still had tears streaming from my lavender pillow-covered eyes.

"What's wrong?" she asked, concerned, quickly moving to my side and lifting the pillow.

"Who's...Kali?" I asked her. It was then that I learned I had been ministered to by a Hindu Deity of whom I had never even *heard*. Kali is revered as the Divine Mother, the ultimate power of creation and destruction. She represents mastery over death, ego, and time, the three things I had prayed to better understand and accept. That's all the proof I needed to confirm a theory I'd always had—that when your intent is sincere, it will be honored. The Divine Energy of The Creator has no restrictions, borders, or judgments. Those are all things we humans have created. Now, exactly, why would we feel the need to hold on to that?

Chapter 11

Paul's Journey

In December of 1999, new tumor growth mushroomed in and around Paul's mouth, making it more difficult for him to eat, talk, or even breathe. One of his doctors told us, "Anything you want to do, do now. Don't even wait until the end of January." Things were looking that bleak. The doctor left the room so we could cry and hold each other, and we got ourselves together and started to walk out of the hospital.

I knew I had to do something to relieve the tension and make Paul laugh, so I turned to him and in my best announcer voice dramatically said, "Paul Lankford! You've just found out you only have weeks to live! What are you going to do next?"

Paul immediately threw his arms in the air and yelled, "I'm going to Disney World!" We were hugging and laughing like idiots, and I'm sure all the people around us were thinking, "That's just so WRONG!" But we didn't care.

Our trip was incredible. All our friends worked together to turn this pilgrimage into the most perfect adventure it could be. One of my friends secretly worked with the travel company to upgrade our cross-country tickets to first class. Another friend upgraded our hotel rooms to concierge level, and still more friends had champagne and fruit baskets sent to our room, along with personalized mouse ears, chocolate covered strawberries and other goodies. They got us into the best restaurants and a Cirque De Soleil show—and we relished every second of being totally spoiled and loved.

When the people working at the Walt Disney World Park realized Paul was one of them, their caring was contagious. They just rolled out the red carpet for him, and we had the most spectacular trip you could imagine. When we got back home, we realized Paul got all this special treatment because both he and I had Disney contacts and a ton of friends in the industry. While it was wonderful for Paul, nothing like that existed for other adults who were terminally ill. There's Make-A-Wish for kids, but we knew of nothing for the grownups.

So, because I had worked at three major theme parks in Southern California—Disneyland brought me out here, then Sea World hired me from Disneyland, then Legoland hired me from Sea World—I talked with my colleagues at the parks, and we established an adult version of Make-A-Wish.

Now when terminally ill parents or grandparents have their physician or social worker call the PR department at one of the parks, they'll get special treatment. They'll be able to get some passes and create happy memories for their loved ones in their final time. That's just one of Paul's legacies.

Dealing with It

Shortly after our return from that great trip, our oncologist assigned us to a psychologist for grief counseling. Because Paul had such a phenomenal attitude about his situation, and he and I openly discussed everything, it kind of blew the psychologist away because he'd never seen people react to death quite like this.

During a session, I'd turn to Paul and say something like, "You've GOT to stop drinking diet soda! That aspartame will KILL you!" The doctor's eyebrows would shoot halfway up his forehead, Paul would start laughing, and the psychologist soon realized our morbid jokes and black humor were the cornerstone of how we were able to handle Paul's deteriorating situation.

The psychologist ended up saying we really didn't need him. He told us, "Yes, you're hurting, and you're sad, but there's nothing I can do for you because you're handling it in a very healthy, functional way." Paul went back to work after our Walt Disney World trip and he continued loving life, squeezing every bit of joy from each day, making every minute count.

My birthday is the first week of June, so in April I started teasing him, saying, "You thought you weren't going to have to buy me a birthday gift this year, didn't you?" Then he surprised ME with a hot air balloon ride. That was one of the things we always wanted to do but just had never done.

The flight over Del Mar was perfect until we started to land. The pilot did not see a fence in the field where we were coming down until we were almost on top of it, and Paul pointed it out. We ended up having to do a crash landing. Our basket dug a deep rut in the field, people were screaming and getting jostled around—it was something right out of a disaster movie. When the balloon finally flopped to a stop and everyone piled out, terrified, Paul walked around, saying, "Well, *I* had nothing to lose!"

It's important to point out we weren't delusional or in denial. We knew what the eventual outcome of Paul's metastasized melanoma was going to be, and it was heartbreaking. But, we were also very aware of the fact that we could control so much just by the attitude we chose to have, and the meaning we chose to give the things that were happening to Paul, and to us. We chose joy.

The *NEWSWEEK* Article

Even though Paul was still going to work, getting all the joy that he could from life, talking to people, making a difference where he could, and our relationship was richer than it had ever been, in the background was the very real knowledge of what lay ahead.

Every day Paul looked in the mirror, and he could see that he was dying bit by bit. He did not want to go the way his father did. Because no topic was taboo for our discussions, he told me maybe we should move to Oregon, where the laws allow assisted suicide, when we got to the end time. Or, maybe he should just crash his truck into a bridge abutment.

We talked about the fact that a big move at that point would be tough, and he wouldn't necessarily die in a truck crash. The bottom line was he wanted to live fully. He wanted to experience every single moment and get all the joy from life he could. However, when the end time came, he wanted to have some control over how he died. He did not want to endure the pain and humiliation of his father's horrible death, or put me, and the rest of his family and friends, through that, either.

Then, in the *Newsweek* Magazine of May 22, 2000, I stumbled across an article titled, "Facing Death on Your Own Terms." It was a huge eye opener, because it told me, for the first time, about a Supreme Court decision from 1997 in which Justice Sandra Day O'Connor wrote: "A patient who is suffering from a terminal illness and who is experiencing great pain has no legal barriers to obtaining medication from qualified physicians, even to the point of causing unconsciousness, and hastening death." (*Vacco v. Quill*, 117 S. Ct. 2293, and *Washington v. Glucksberg*, 117 S. Ct. 2258)

My brother Jeff and Paul's sister Debbie were both attorneys. We immediately gave them this information, and they did the research to confirm this decision was true. Despite all our questions to the oncologist and other specialists, no one had ever said anything at all about this option.

When we brought this article to our next oncologist visit, the doctor just crossed his arms across his chest and said, "I will not be involved with anything like this, and I do not discuss this with my patients." He also refused to refer us to Hospice, even though we just wanted general information at that point.

So, even though we hit a brick wall there, we knew the law was on our side when the end time came. Paul was incredibly relieved, and continued going in to work every day. His attitude improved remarkably, and he could release the fear that had been hanging over his head. Now, he knew he could have some control over how he closed the sacred circle of his life.

Paul the Superhero

Paul was very conscious of wanting to take care of things for me. He gathered up a bunch of his old stuff and we had a garage sale, which he jokingly called his "Going out of Business" sale.

Meanwhile, he was becoming something of a superhero at Disneyland. His fellow employees respected him even more because he stayed so positive, and because he continued to pull his weight and do his job, never taking advantage of his situation.

One particular incident has become legend. It happened when a woman who was physically challenged was waiting for an overdue bus that would take people from the Disneyland parking lot to the Park entrance. Other guests were getting on regular buses while this woman continued to wait for the specially equipped vehicle. She became angry, and moved into the center of the loading area so no buses could pull in or out. Other Park Cast Members implored her to stop blocking the pickup area. She refused, so they sent in Paul.

Paul walked over to the woman and said, "Howdy, Ma'am, what seems to be the problem?"

"Just because I'm handicapped, I shouldn't have to wait for a bus," she snapped.

"Lady," Paul said, pointing to the large gauze patch on his face covering his wound, "I'm dying, but that doesn't give me the right to mess up everyone else's day!" The woman, shocked, retreated to the sidewalk, to the cheers and applause of the on-looking guests and Cast Members.

While Paul was basking in the love and respect of his co-workers, everything in our personal life, too, was so much richer. Around dusk we'd start yelling, "Sunset! Sunset!" We'd jump in the car and rush to the beach, where we'd hold hands and watch the sun sink into the ocean. Everything was so intense, wonderful, and meaningful. We'd work through Paul's bucket list and start another one, and we had frequent talks about closure.

My own spiritual belief is we all come here to do something. We have some kind of a mission—something we're supposed to learn or accomplish. Paul and I talked a lot about what he felt was his own mission. I asked him why he continued to endure this excruciating pain and humiliation as his face slowly rotted away in front of his eyes. What was he hanging around to still try and do?

Paul realized he was hoping to reconcile his mother and brother. His mother was mentally ill, and through her irrational behavior had totally alienated his older brother. The two hadn't spoken in 20 years. Paul's previous attempts to bring them together hadn't worked because his mother wouldn't hear of it, and his brother was pretty stubborn too. The situation saddened him deeply.

In October, nearly a year after one doctor had told us we might just have a few weeks left, Paul's oncologist finally referred us to hospice. The hospice team was truly phenomenal. Because Paul was still going to work as many days a week as he could to keep a sense of normalcy in his life, his hospice nurse, May Bull, and social worker, Julie Thomas, very thoughtfully scheduled their visits around his hours.

They both immediately understood us, and our bizarre sense of humor. They also were sensitive to the challenges we were having with Paul's mother. She would call him up almost daily and say, "How can you do this to me! You don't care what happens to me! You're just going to die and leave me all alone! If you went to this clinic in Tijuana you'd be fine!"

Her volatile, delusional outbursts were a huge drain on Paul. May and Julie were wonderful in understanding and offering Paul support. At this point, the tumors were growing pretty quickly. New growths had now broken through the skin on his face, and Paul had lost about 50 pounds because the tumors were affecting his jaw, making it increasingly difficult for him to eat, chew, and swallow. As the disease progressed, the pain level was becoming more of a challenge because of Paul's morphine allergy.

At this point, after a couple of months of working with the hospice team and continuing to commute to Disneyland, Paul wanted to discuss the *Newsweek* article and find out exactly what his options were.

The Meeting

During the next hospice home care visit, Paul and I brought out the *Newsweek* article, and told May and Julie we wanted to find out how this applied to Paul. They immediately set up a visit with Dr. Mike Frederich, a physician with San Diego Hospice. The three of them were terrific. First, they listened to Paul's fears about reliving his father's horrific experience, and how he seriously had considered a move to Oregon, or a suicide attempt with his truck.

Then, one by one, all of Paul's fears were quelled as Dr. Mike walked Paul through several options he had with hospice. The one that immediately put Paul at ease was controlled sedation. He would choose the day he decided to admit himself to hospice, and would then receive a sedative every half hour until he entered into a gentle, pain-free sleep.

At any time, he could decide to stop the process and come back to full consciousness. Every aspect of the decision was entirely under his control. Because he had signed an advance directive the previous year, Paul knew that after he lost consciousness, as he wished, he would not receive any hydration or nutrition intravenously.

Because Paul's pain level was steadily increasing, Dr. Mike authorized a Dilaudid pump to be inserted subcutaneously. We both realized this was a very definite indicator that his time was growing short.

That was a tough meeting. We asked very direct questions, and Dr. Mike gave us very direct and honest answers. It was painful to hear, but it gave Paul such a sense of peace because of the dignity with which he was treated, and because the honesty and respect were so healing. Dr. Mike told Paul that because he was so healthy from the neck down, it would take his body about three weeks to shut down if he decided to choose controlled sedation.

After the team left, Paul told me, "I want to be here as long as I can. But when I decide to go, it's not going to take me three weeks."

After that intense but comforting meeting, Paul's sense of well-being, control and humor came back with a vengeance. We watched a Discovery Channel special on the Mayan pyramids, and the narrator said archeologists had deciphered the writing on the temples to mean the world was going to end in 2012. Paul laughed and turned to me, saying, "I'm just getting out while the getting's good!"

Shortly after Paul received the terminal diagnosis, I had asked in prayer to know when we were truly getting toward Paul's end time. Immediately I was shown a much thinner version of him. When he physically began to resemble that image I'd seen 18 months earlier, I made the decision to leave the corporate world, and concentrate on taking care of this incredible man I loved so dearly. Actually, it really wasn't that tough a decision at all. I resigned my high-powered Legoland executive position at the end of October 2000.

Sacred Sedona Journey

As the spreading melanoma continued to take more and more of Paul's face, it was increasingly evident that anything we wanted to do, we'd better start doing. During our marriage, Paul had shared Yosemite with me, and the power and sacredness of those mountains and valleys immediately took up residence in my heart. Just about every year we were together, we spent at least a few days camping in Curry Village, exploring trails, meditating in the groves, and snapping hundreds of pictures.

It was easy for me to see how this spectacular place had brought him such peace after his father's death.

I had found a similar resonance in Sedona on several visits before I'd met Paul, and he and I frequently spoke about visiting the mountains and red rocks that had called so clearly to me. Now, I was driven by an overwhelmingly urgent need to share this sacred place with the man I loved before he died.

We planned our Sedona trip the first week of November. Paul was so sick the hospice social worker and nurse who had been lovingly working with us told us honestly there was an excellent chance Paul would die on the trip. He felt the same urgency to visit Sedona that I did, so he wasn't deterred. Julie and May gave us the contact numbers for hospice team members in both Phoenix and Sedona.

As I started booking our flight, rental car, and hotel reservations a few weeks in advance, I discovered a dormitory at the Hopi Cultural Center, about 90 miles out of Flagstaff. Even though it would be quite a drive, I wanted to have Paul immersed in the powerful, sacred energy of the Hopi Nation, and booked a room.

A late fall snowstorm on the eve of our trip shut the roads around Flagstaff, and Hopi Nation was suddenly inaccessible. I had to select a second hotel quickly and randomly. I closed my eyes, asked for guidance, and called one from a list that popped up on Google. They had space, so I made the reservation and finished packing.

Our flight from San Diego to Phoenix was hell for Paul. His pain and anxiety continued on the two-hour drive to Sedona, and he was unable to get comfortable enough for even a quick nap. He never complained, but occasionally a soft moan escaped from his cancer-ravaged lips.

It was late afternoon when we finally arrived in Sedona, and I immediately drove right to Bell Rock, one of the major energy vortex spots. Paul was so wiped out at that point he couldn't admire the magnificent tower of red rock jutting toward the crystal clear sky. I helped him struggle out of the car into the nippy desert air, and supported him as he took a few wobbly steps.

What slowly began to happen still brings tears to my eyes nine years later. At first, we just stood there in the shadow of the rock. Paul raised his head to look at it then moved a step closer. I could feel him begin to straighten up. He took a few more steps holding on to my arm, and stopped again to gaze at the magnificent natural structure. He didn't say a word, but then again, he didn't have to. His breathing gradually changed from the short, shallow gasps of a person in pain to slower, deeper breaths. The powerful energy of this magical place was taking hold, and I could feel the strength slowly starting to come back into his gaunt, stooped frame. A sacred healing had begun.

We walked the circle around the entire rock, and by the time we'd made the final part of the rotation, Paul's stride was confident and purposeful. His transformation in body, mind, and spirit in just half an hour was truly miraculous.

"This place is GREAT!" he said with more enthusiasm than he'd been able to muster in weeks. "We DEFINITELY had to come here!"

"I cannot *believe* how strong you're looking," I said as I hugged him. "We can come back here tomorrow, and check out some other vortexes, but now we should probably find our hotel before it gets dark."

"Could I have the keys?" he asked as we approached the car.

"Honey, if you feel up to it, absolutely you can drive!" He hadn't been behind the wheel in weeks—this was definitely a huge shift in his energy. I was so happy for this break in the clouds. Even though Paul's lips and a third of his face had been lost to the cancer, I could tell he was smiling, too.

Our last-minute substitution hotel was on one of Sedona's main drags, so it was easy to find. Paul pulled up to the lobby and I ran in to register. I was a jumble of emotions—exultation at Paul's amazing transformation, exhaustion at the grueling trip, and the constant sorrow that had veiled my heart since we'd first received the grim diagnosis. But as I walked up to the front desk, I began to feel...great. Peaceful. Happy. Mindful. Safe.

"Welcome to Kokopelli Inn," the man at the counter said in a deep, friendly voice. His dark eyes smiled, and ink black hair hung below his shoulders. "How may I help you?"

"Reservations for Lankford, please," I said. As the man consulted his computer, I noticed a newspaper article displayed in a plastic frame on the counter. I gasped. The Hopi Nation had just purchased this hotel; it was their first off-reservation venture into the tourism industry. A glorious shiver ran up my spine. Paul and I didn't need to drive all the way to the Hopi— the Hopi had come to us! Once again, the perfection of universal synchronicity wrapped me in its loving warmth and reassurance.

"You have a good room," the man said. "We've done a lot of work here at the Inn, and it's very comfortable now."

"Did you smudge the rooms?" I asked. In First Person traditions, "smudging" is the ceremonial burning of certain herbs, frequently sage, cedar or sweetgrass, to cleanse a person or location of any harmful energies, feelings or thoughts. The clerk allowed himself a smile, and nodded.

He was right—the room was good. Even though there was a Jacuzzi in the corner, Paul and I both quickly collapsed into bed. It had been a huge day.

I lay next to Paul, my eyes closed, silently sending my gratitude to Spirit for the miracles that had been sent to us. First, not only did Paul survive the trip to Sedona, but also thanks to the healing energy around Bell Rock, he was positively thriving. It seemed as if the months had been turned back, and his old spirit was rekindled. Then there was the miracle of "coincidentally" choosing the first and only Hopi-owned hotel off reservation land. How fantastic it felt to be lying in that energy, feeling the sacred peace and power. I prayed "Thank you, God, for all these blessings…."

My prayer was cut short when Paul playfully put the sheet up to my face, touched my cheek with it, then put it back around my waist. I opened my eyes to tell him to stop it—and saw he was fast asleep. The sheet had never moved. It appeared we weren't quite done with miracles for the day.

Immediately I invoked the prayer of Christ Light and Protection and asked to understand what had just happened. My answer was a quick vision of a white owl, and the hollow, echoing sound of something very large flying past my left ear and into the void behind me.

Then I understood.

The white owl is a guardian of the door between the spiritual and physical worlds. It touched my cheek with its wing then flew back into the shadows, to let me know Paul would be given more time here on Earth. It was a blessing and a promise. As it turned out, we had the huge gift of three more months together, when before, we were only given days. It was a good room.

Counting Down

The Sedona trip and the energy Paul sucked in from those vortexes made such a difference that he defied all the odds and survived through Christmas and New Year's to January 2001, when we actually got to do the preview of Disney's California Adventure.

The two days we spent there were so rich and bittersweet. This was a Cast Member-only preview, a private party for the people who worked for Disney, so we could not go three or four feet without an old friend coming over to hug him. He had worked at the park for nearly three decades, so everyone knew and loved him, and it was such a sacred opportunity for him to say thank you and goodbye to everyone. It meant the world to him.

By this time, Paul had also won his fight to change the Disney dress code. Throughout the new Park, it was a thrill to see Cast Members wearing wide-brimmed hats to shield their faces from the blistering southern California sun.

The days after that milestone in his Disney career, Paul began an emotionally wrenching self-documentation of his rapidly deteriorating condition. He took pictures of the growing, gaping holes in his chin and cheek, and told me,

"Hold on to these photos. You're going to need them." Somehow, he knew his story would live long after his death, and he wanted to make sure people understood every part of his journey.

At this point, he had pretty much stopped eating because his teeth were too loose and painful to chew, and he could only open his jaw about half an inch. His body was looking more and more like the vision I'd been given in order to gauge his remaining time. His breathing was becoming more difficult as tumors pushed against his throat. Several times a day, he taped a new wadded-up gauze pad under his open wound to catch the pus oozing from it.

It was the night of February 8, 2001, that I awakened to his screams. During one of his muscle spasms, caused by the toxic level of Dilaudid in his system, Paul punched himself in the face, and caught his thumb in the festering hole where his cheek had been. I sprang to his side of the bed and helped him untangle his hand, then held him tightly as we both sobbed.

"I can't do this anymore," he gasped, his body twitching in pain. "I'm just exhausted."

That morning, as he stared at his rotting face in the mirror, he took a deep breath and told me, "It is a good day to die. Go ahead and call hospice." I got Julie on the phone, and she said she and May would meet us at the facility in an hour. I told her Paul wanted to take one last cruise on the San Diego harbor, so we'd be there later that afternoon.

Paul told me to call a locksmith, and we waited while all the locks to the house were changed in case his mother had copied our keys. He didn't want her coming in while we were gone and taking all his things. This was a very real concern of his because she was that unstable.

During our two-hour boat ride, Paul held me while I sobbed, and gently admonished me to "Stop that!" While I was heartbroken, I totally respected the fact that this was Paul's decision. He was so peaceful, focused, and calm, even when we finally arrived on the hospice grounds.

The fact that he was able to walk into the facility, and then tour the grounds, turned out to be a serious problem for some of the hospice staff members. Paul was so comfortable with the whole thing he even had his brother take a picture of the two of us on his hospice room balcony. In the photo, while my eyes are red and puffy from crying, his are so loving and calm. If he still would have had a face, it would have been smiling. Instead, you can just see his jaw and teeth.

His sense of humor remained intact, too. As his nurse was helping us get settled in Paul's room, Paul noticed a stack of CDs on a shelf. He pulled out a Perry Como CD, and said to the nurse, "You know, I'm not dead YET!" She was horrified, while May and Julie laughed right along with him.

Then, there was a touching moment as the two women, who had been so important to Paul, told him what an honor it had been to work with him. While both of them, and I, started to cry, it was Paul who comforted all of us. There was no doubt in his mind that he was making the right decision. His sense of peace, purpose, and gratitude for a life well lived was unwavering.

After he was admitted to the hospice facility, Paul stopped the oral prophylactic antibiotics, and the nurse began a drip of the powerful sedative Versed. Per Dr. Mike's orders, the attending nurse was to increase the dose of the sedative every half hour until Paul entered a peaceful, pain-free sleep.

Half an hour passed after he received his first dose, then an hour, then an hour and a half. I went in search of his nurse, and found her at the desk. When I asked her why she had not been back to the room, she stuck out her chin and said accusingly, "I'm not going to help you kill your husband!"

I was shocked, but more than that, I was extremely protective of Paul. This man was my best friend, my soul mate, and the love of my life. It broke my heart that I was losing him, but I knew, on every level, Paul's decision was the right one. This was something we had researched, prayed about, discussed with doctors, lawyers, ministers, and psychologists.

We'd talked, laughed, cried, accepted, adjusted and chosen—this certainly was NOT a decision Paul had entered into lightly.

The fact that one woman thought she could unilaterally overrule the Supreme Court was ludicrous, and her behavior, which defied the doctor's orders, was professionally unethical and unacceptable. But, more than that, her rage, fear, and judgment created such a toxic energy around her that I knew I had to keep her away from Paul as he completed his sacred circle of life.

Instead of fighting with her, I continued my silent prayers for strength and grace as I returned to Paul's room, and crawled in bed with him. I held him as he drifted in and out of sleep, talking with him, thanking him for sharing his life with me, and telling him I loved him, and I released him. I called on all the spiritual strength I had to keep the energy in his room positive, loving, and calm during his transition.

At one point a different nurse came into the room with a catheter. I sent her away—I had promised Paul he wouldn't have to endure that indignity as long as he was conscious. He even refused the bedside urinal, asking me to half-carry him into the private bathroom several times.

During our last such trip, at about 3 a.m. Saturday morning, Paul was only able to take tiny, shuffling steps as I supported him. After needing several minutes to go only a few feet, Paul stopped and said in a groggy voice, "I feel like Tim Conway!" He was referring to one of Tim's comedy sketches about an annoying old man who slowly shuffled across the stage. Paul wanted to make me laugh with that quip. He did.

I repeatedly asked him if he was sure this is what he wanted to do, and he nodded and squeezed my hand. I helped him back into bed, and he continued to drift in and out of sleep as I held him, talking to him, loving him, letting him go.

Finally, the shift changed, and the new nursing team immediately got everything back on track. Paul received a few more doses of the sedative and gently drifted into a deep, pain-free sleep. His comfort and dignity were maintained to the end.

Saturday and Sunday, as Paul's body was shutting down, a steady parade of friends and family arrived to help keep watch. We told funny Paul stories, we laughed and cried together, we prayed, and chanted, and played his favorite music. We talked about how the world was a better place because he had been here. All the while, we kept the energy in the room positive, peaceful, and sacred.

Per Paul's prediction, he didn't require three weeks—but only three days. A few weeks before, I had a dream that I wouldn't be by his side when he died. He and I had discussed this, and we both made our peace with that.

By Monday morning, I was exhausted, and Paul's sister Debbie drove me home to shower and catch a quick nap. We hadn't even made it back to the house when her cell phone rang with the news. While Paul's brother was by his side, holding one hand, and his mother was on his other side, holding his other hand, Paul finally crossed over. With his last breath, he achieved the closure he was seeking—he brought the two of them together in a sacred circle.

It was a perfect end to a beautiful, joyful life.

It turned out to be just the beginning, though, of the emotional, volatile, and ethical debate about controlled sedation as an option for end-of-life. In the resulting hospice studies devoted to the issue on a national scale, and what went wrong in Paul's specific case, one of the arguments was that patients who were able to walk into the facility shouldn't be administered controlled sedation. It was suggested that maybe this option be limited to a patient's home so as not to disrupt the hospice facility staff.

If this had been the case when Paul made the difficult decision to choose controlled sedation, God only knows what kind of legal and law enforcement precautions we would have had to impose to keep his mother from breaking into the house and dragging him off to that clinic in Mexico.

I completely respect the fact that some people, including hospice staff, might have religious disagreements with this legal choice. Bottom line, though, they then have an ethical, moral, and professional responsibility to remove themselves from the case.

Not only is this a patient's legal and moral right—it's also, as I sincerely hope I've conveyed, NOT a decision that a patient and family enter into lightly. This is NOT assisted suicide, or a Kevorkian-like "escape." There is no death-inducing pharmaceutical administered to the patient. Rather, it's providing a pain-relieving sedative slowly, in measured doses, allowing the patient to change his or her mind at any point during the procedure and reverse the process.

No one is "killed." Rather, medications that were prolonging a life screeching to a painful close are stopped, and the patient is allowed just to go to sleep.

I was sharing Paul's story with a friend a few years later, and she burst into tears. At first, I was afraid I had offended her in some way. It was just the opposite. Her own father had recently died a slow, torturous death from emphysema. As his fluid-filled lungs reflexively struggled to take in air, his doctors kept reducing the amount of morphine they were giving him so he would continue to fight to breathe.

Had she and her father known about the Supreme Court decision, my friend said, her dad could have gently, painlessly and fearlessly entered into his final sleep instead of enduring an additional agonizing two weeks in Intensive Care.

While it is always emotionally draining for me to relive Paul's death, I understand that it is important to share the information he so carefully and deliberately preserved. That is why I have spoken to thousands of people, including nursing students, doctoral candidates, social workers, chaplains, nurses and doctors. I share the pictures he took, and a "Cliff Notes" version of his life, to help put a face and a heart to a case number. I wrote an article that appeared in INSIGHTS, the magazine of the National Hospice and Palliative Care Organization. The attending doctor's sidebar article, "A Physician's Perspective on End of Life Care," appears in the back of this book.

If retelling my husband's experience can help other people like my friend's dying father, and the end-of-life caregivers who will encounter similar situations over and over, then it is all worthwhile, and a true testament to Paul's loving, generous and joyful nature.

A quick postscript: I shared this story at the National Conference of Hospice and Palliative Care in Las Vegas a few years ago, and a woman with tear-filled eyes came up to me at the end of the presentation. At that point, I was emotionally spent, so I didn't even think to ask her name.

The gist of the woman's story, though, was that her 19-year-old nephew just got a summer job at Disneyland, and was looking forward to getting a deep, dark tan. His second day on the job, his mom noticed he was slathering on sun block. She was thrilled, and asked him what had changed his mind.

"Mom," he said breathlessly. "There was this guy who used to work at Disneyland! His name was Paul..." At that point, the woman and I were BOTH sobbing! The point of the story is that sharing tough information can save young lives, and can help bring a sacred peace to end-of-life care. Paul's legacy lives on!

Chapter 12

Love Never Dies

Even though I knew spiritually that Paul didn't really LEAVE-leave, and he had just shifted energies, I was still heartbroken that he wasn't there for me anymore in a physical, huggable body. After a lifetime of feeling I had to hide my intuitive gifts, I finally had found a man who respected and encouraged my abilities, and then I lost him to cancer.

He wasn't about to stop making me smile, though.

The first three mornings after his death, the television, which had been on a news channel when I shut it off the previous night, was switched to the Disney Channel. VERY funny!

My dear friend from Florida came to be with me. Kathy Echroll and I met when I moved to Miami to work, and we immediately bonded over café Cubano and our love for, and frustration with, working at a TV station. She was delighted with my way of being in the world, and was quite intuitive herself.

She'd met Paul before we married, and immediately approved. Kathy realized how difficult it had been for me to try to ignore my psychic abilities during my marriage to Ed, and she was thrilled I'd found such a great guy who loved me completely and unconditionally. She, too, deeply grieved his untimely death.

The day she arrived, we drove to Doggie Beach, a part of the San Diego coastline Paul and I had walked frequently. We always loved to watch the dogs dashing into the waves to catch Frisbees, body surfing with their people, and lining up to "mark" tufts of seaweed littering the sand.

As Kathy and I talked and cried in the car, we had the radio softly playing a Top 40 station. Suddenly we stopped talking, and just stared at each other. The station, for some "inexplicable" reason, had just broken format, and was playing the Norman Greenbaum song, *Spirit in the Sky*.

> *"When I die and they lay me to rest*
> *Gonna go to the place that's the best*
> *When I lay me down to die*
> *Going up to the Spirit in the sky...."*
> © Great Honesty Music

The song was over 30 years old, and we were listening to a contemporary music station. It was simply *impossible* for that particular number to be playing on the air.

We cracked up. Coincidence? I think *not*.

But, the MOST blatant connection—at least a few months after Paul died—he stole straight from the bittersweet song, *As I Lay Me Down* by Sophie B. Hawkins. It's a hauntingly beautiful melody with an equally moving story. I read somewhere that she wrote the entire thing in minutes, on a napkin, when she felt a sudden strong connection with her late father.

The song talks about a February morning—Paul died February 12—and says how she's remembering things he said to her. When she lies down to sleep, she prays he'll hold her dear, and she'll wake up happy. Check it out on YouTube; it's just wonderful.

When I awoke one morning, I suddenly felt extremely happy for the first time since Paul's death months before. Then I realized I felt a warm, gentle finger touching my third eye, but "no one" was there. No one, that is, except my loving husband literally in touch with me from the spirit side. It was a powerful moment, and truly it shifted my deep heart sorrow into gratitude for the near-perfect decade we'd been given together. Of course it still hurt terribly, but at least I had physical confirmation that the worlds of the living and the dead literally connect.

Circle of Life

Disneyland had been Paul's life for nearly 30 years. It was only fitting that it was also such a sacred part of his death.

For his funeral, dozens of his friends met at the Disneyland parking lot and boarded buses for the 40-minute trip to the San Juan Capistrano campus of the Crystal Cathedral. Paul and I picked that spot because it was midway between Anaheim and San Diego.

Patrick Alo and Lindsay Schnebly, close friends I'd worked with at Disneyland, helped me decorate with balloons and hand out tiny bubble-blowing vials. There were spontaneous clouds of iridescent bubbles floating around the church throughout the service. We all shared funny Paul stories, and then enjoyed a great meal. It was a beautiful, meaningful sendoff for a dear soul who was adored—and deeply missed.

His loving, gentle presence was felt by everyone at the celebration.

Of Angels and Pelicans

Both my brothers were able to shift hectic schedules to fly from Pennsylvania to San Diego to be there with me to scatter Paul's ashes. Jim Antrim, former Sea World curator and another close friend, graciously offered to take the three of us, and my Miami friend Kathy, out to sea in his boat for our ceremony. Jim's beautiful wife Jennine completed our little group.

We were solemn at the start of the ride as Jim pointed the boat up the coast, toward our beloved Doggie Beach. Before long, though, we were all making bad jokes and telling funny

Paul stories, finding comfort in our laughter and connectedness.

When our special stretch of beach was in sight, Jim cut the engines. A pelican, Paul's favorite bird, fluttered down onto the water several yards from the boat. I started tossing tuberoses, Paul's favorite flower, into the waves. A second pelican dove into the ocean on the other side of the boat, then surfaced and floated there, watching us.

"That's odd," Jim said. "They don't normally hang around people like this." At that point, a THIRD pelican joined the aquatic flotilla, forming a perfect triangle around our boat. All three birds stayed in formation while we said a few words and emptied the baggie full of Paul's ashes into the sea.

"I've just never seen anything like that," Jim said again, shaking his head at the pelicans. My little brother Jeffrey and I exchanged glances. He and I had frequent talks about psychic and metaphysical phenomena, and he realized this unique display of pelican solidarity was deeply significant to me. He raised his disposable camera, and snapped a picture of one of the birds.

It was a lovely day—sad, but sacred. There was finality to everything, and a formal closure to the deliriously happy, yet cruelly brief, chapter of my life as Paul's wife. There were more tears, stories and laughs as Jim piloted the boat back to the dock.

It was the first time my two brothers and I had been together—all three of us at once—since my Christmas trip home the year Ed and I divorced. We mugged for Kathy's camera. We tortured each other with old sibling rivalries. We updated one another on what was happening in our lives. Both brothers had four kids each, and took turns sharing the latest adventures of my eight brilliant and gorgeous nieces and nephews. It was a tender reconnection that had to end way too soon.

A week later, after both brothers had returned to Pennsylvania and Kathy was back in Miami, I got a late night call from Jeff. "Ah, Jonna Raesie," he said, using my nickname from childhood, "I have something here that is completely out of my realm, but I know it's in yours."

"What do you mean?" I asked.

"That picture I took of the pelican from the boat? There's something else showing up in it."

"Something else? Like WHAT?"

"Ah...I just e-mailed it to you. Check it out and tell me what YOU think!"

I ran into my den and clicked on Jeff's e-mail. I downloaded the picture in question, and did a double-take.

There, in color, was the unmistakable arch of an angel's wing, partially transparent but clearly visible. I could even make out rows of feathers curving around the sweep of white.

"Jeff," I said in hushed tones, "I'm clearly seeing an angel." I had goose bumps on top of goose bumps.

"Yep," he said. "That's what I saw, too. But I'm a LAWYER. I don't believe this is POSSIBLE."

"Jeffrix," I said, using his childhood nickname, too. "Welcome to my world. If anyone would have an angel show up for their burial at sea, it would be Paul!"

To this day, nearly a decade later, the image still brings me such a sense of peace, gratitude, and joy.

Yogananda's Healing Touch

I frequently visited the Center for Self-Realization in Encinitas, where Paramahansa Yogananda wrote his book, *Autobiography of a Yogi*. The grounds are spectacular, and overlook the Pacific. Right before Paul died I fell down some stairs, broke my left foot in three places, and wrenched my shoulder. I realized immediately that was God saying, "Stop running around like a crazy person planning Paul's funeral, and just sit on the couch with your husband and hold his hand."

And that's exactly how Paul and I spent his last two weeks. After Paul's death, a friend and I decided to go to the Self-Realization Church one Sunday morning. My foot was healing rapidly, but my shoulder was still quite painful, and I couldn't raise my arm. At the beginning of the service, the entire congregation chants in unison for a magnificently powerful raising of energy, and then the congregation sits in silent meditation for a few minutes. Shortly after the meditation began, the person sitting behind me reached forward and put his or her warm hand on my sore shoulder. What a friendly, caring greeting, I thought, and I sincerely appreciated the gesture. I continued to meditate with my eyes closed while the nice person's hand stayed on my shoulder.

As the meditation part of the service ended, I turned around to thank the kind person. And—there was no one sitting there. And—I still felt the invisible but very warm and comforting hand on my shoulder! Guess I don't need to tell you, when we walked outside the church and I tried raising my arm, my shoulder was completely healed. Miracles are all around us, waiting for us to accept them! Open your mind, open your heart, and open your world to the magnificent possibilities waiting for you to claim them. As Richard Bach said in *Illusions, Adventures of a Reluctant Messiah,* "Argue for your limitations and sure enough, they're yours."

Special Delivery!

A year to the day after Paul's death, I was being promoted from Minister with the Universal Brotherhood Movement to Minister-Director. In my new position, I would have the authority to ordain other ministers into the non-denominational group, which requires members to take a vow to be of service to humanity.

Even though Paul didn't have specific spiritual beliefs, he respected the fact that I did. I was feeling a bit disappointed that he wouldn't be there for the little ceremony, which we were having on a bluff right next to Yogananda's Center for Self-Realization. I knew Paul would be happy for me, and if he were still alive, he'd be there to support me.

The President of Universal Brotherhood (UB) at the time, Rev. Gregory Possman, was officiating. Irma, another UB minister, was also being promoted. She and I sat on a cement bench on a cliff overlooking the Pacific Ocean. It was a breathtakingly gorgeous spot.

Gregory led us in prayer as we rededicated ourselves to our spiritual work. For the portion of the service where he placed the violet mantle of the church over our shoulders, we had our eyes closed in silent meditation. At the conclusion of the ceremony, I opened my eyes, and was delighted to find Gregory had placed a beautiful yellow wildflower next to me on the bench. Yellow flowers are my favorite. I picked up the bloom and sniffed its delicate fragrance.

"What color flower did you get?" I asked Irma.

"I didn't *get* a flower," she said. She and I both turned to look quizzically at Gregory.

"I didn't put that flower there," he said to me. "I thought you brought it with you!"

"No, I didn't." I said slowly. "And it definitely wasn't there when we sat down!"

Excited now, all three of us scattered to see if that particular type of flower was growing anywhere in the cliff-top park. There were no other flowers like that one. After searching for several minutes, I could only reach one conclusion.

"I'm pretty sure this was a gift from Paul," I said. "I know that's not 'logical,' in the traditional sense, but it's the only explanation I can possibly see. And believe me, stranger things have happened!"

We all laughed, and I sent Paul a very sincere and heart-felt thank you. He was there for me after all. Like I said—embrace the miracles. The more you acknowledge them and express gratitude for them, the more you'll experience them. I promise!

Chapter 13
Moving On

One of Paul's sweet quirks was always putting glow-in-the-dark stars on the ceiling of the bedroom. Hotels, friends' homes, the three bedrooms in our little home—Paul enhanced all of them with at least a smattering of invisible-by-day, brilliant-by-night decorations. In fact, during a party we hosted at the house, one of my earthy Disneyland friends loved the ceiling stars, but thought we should do more.

"You should put stars on the toilet seat so you can find it at night," Matt said, trying to shock me.

"Really?" I replied. "You mean like 'The Big and Little Drippers?'" I won that one!

Fast forward past our move to a big rental house in San Diego when Sea World hired me away from Disney, to the time right after Paul's death on February 12th, 2001.

All logical sources say you're supposed to wait for at least a year after a spouse dies before making any drastic changes in your life. Logic, never being one of my strong suits, went completely out the window when the landlord gently let me know he planned to raise the rent dramatically the first of the following year.

With the gift of Paul's life insurance, I was able to pony up a healthy deposit on a home, so a realtor and I set about looking for a little place for me to buy. The day she showed me several, none of them "felt" right, and I could feel her impatience. Then, we turned onto Calle Valperizo in Carlsbad, very close to the Deepak Chopra Center. Mmmmm. GREAT vibes already.

The owners, a hip young couple with a lively little boy, invited us right in. Corner unit on a cul-de-sac, right on a wide, lush greenbelt with 40-foot trees. Tons of big closets. Fireplaces in the living room and the master. A cool retro black and white kitchen with a huge pass-through window into the adjoining tiled dining room. A custom wood trellis over the back patio, with a flowering passion vine winding through the open slats of the trellis roof. WAY cool.

"There are three bedrooms and two bathrooms upstairs," the realtor said, leading us up the steps. That's when I saw it. The dad, who was a graphic designer, had painted their son's room a deep cobalt blue. And, there, on the ceiling, was an out-of-this-world panorama that made me gasp.

Artist that he was, the dad recreated, in perfect scale, our entire solar system. Intricately painted Styrofoam balls for each planet were suspended from the ceiling, all in their rightful orbit. Asteroid belts were painted directly on the ceiling, along with multiple galaxies of glowing stars. I couldn't speak. It was perfect. And I KNEW this was going to be my new home; and somehow Paul was pulling the strings to make it happen. It was like his version of little glow-in-the-dark stars on the ceiling, but on steroids. For the first time since the realtor and I started looking, I felt at peace.

"Of course I'll paint over that bedroom...," the dad started to say as we came back down the stairs.

"NO!" I interrupted him. "That's my new global office!" We all laughed.

We shook hands; the realtor submitted our offer to their realtor, and then—a glitch. A woman had actually submitted an offer about two days before ours, and she decided she wanted the house. She had a 60-day escrow.

"We'll just have to find something else," my realtor said, but I knew we had already found it. "Galaxy House" was going to be mine.

The next few weeks the realtor pushed me hard to settle for another property. She cajoled, turned up quite late to showings, and was increasingly short-tempered. She even jumped the gun, and sent out a direct mail piece to clients saying I had actually bought one of the other townhouses she was pushing me to buy. But, I "knew," with every cell in my body, I was going to get Galaxy House, despite the growing impatience of the realtor.

And—of course—the other buyer dropped out two days before escrow was to close.

Within two weeks—I opted for a VERY short escrow—the house was mine. I moved in December 22nd; it was the perfect bittersweet Christmas gift from Paul.

Professional Courtesy, Aunt to Ant

My new San Diego County condo was lovely in every respect except one—it was apparently constructed in the middle of a humongous anthill. I learned from my neighbors that EVERYONE suffered ant infestations. The ubiquitous creatures didn't just turn up for picnics, but for every part of life in our little La Costa community.

Through my decades vacationing in this part of the galaxy, I've learned that everything—EVERYTHING—has a consciousness. From parliaments to presidents to pine trees to paper clips, absolutely every part of creation, seen and unseen, known and unknown, has a sentient element. Call on it, and you are connected.

When I saw my first "condo ant," I sat down with it and had a little chat. I started, as I do with all things, by thinking the All-Purpose Affirmation. Then I took a deep breath, and began the conversation.

"I don't want to kill you," I told it, "but I don't want to be overrun by your tribe, either. Let's make a deal. This inside space is mine, and the outside is yours. I'll respect your space and won't hurt you if you respect mine, and stay outdoors."

The ant wiggled its tiny antennae and crawled onto the piece of paper I lay in front of it. I took the paper, and the ant, out onto the patio, and set the paper down. The ant crawled off and into the soil, presumably to confer with other anty bodies.

For the next four and a half years, I never sprayed my condo with pesticides, and I never saw another ant inside. When I was putting fresh nectar out for the hummingbirds, I would leave a little splash of the sugar water for the ants. Everyone was happy—there was no need to antagonize one another.

Great Web Site

And, speaking of bugs...one morning I stepped out the front door to get the newspaper, and discovered overnight that a huge garden spider had spun a four-foot web from the roof of the garage across my front entryway to the patio wall. It was truly a spectacular work of art in perfect symmetry, and it completely blocked my path to the curb.

Again, I "went up" in consciousness and connected with the pewter gray web master.

"Your work is just lovely," I told her, "but you put it where I can't get out of my house. I honor you, but you can't block my pathway. Please go up on the garage roof. I'm going to get a broom and take down your web, and I don't want to hurt you."

I could have sworn the spider rolled her eyes—all eight of them—before she scooted over one of the anchoring strands, and headed up to the roof of the garage. I returned with the broom and reluctantly swept away what probably took yards of silk and many hours to create.

When I stepped outside the next morning to get the paper, I had to stop and laugh. My intrepid arachnid friend had respun her web—but THIS time, she created it sideways, so I could walk under it without stooping. Well done, Charlotte! Well done.

Grandma Says "Hi"

After I moved into my cute little condo, I switched to a holistic dentist whose office was much nearer my new home. On my first visit there, Bonnie, the hygienist, who was just being polite as she was starting to clean my teeth, asked me what I did. I decided to go for it.

"I'm a writer," I said, "And I'm also an intuitive consultant."

"REAL-ly," she said, with exaggerated deference. "So where's that box of stuff I'm supposed to send to my sister?"

"It's under the sink," I answered immediately. She put down the little mirror and stared at me.

"The box of stuff for your sister is under the sink," I repeated. The woman looked a bit flustered, but gamely kept talking as she prodded and probed my gums. Since it had become, of necessity, a one-way conversation at that point, she continued talking, and eventually said something about her late grandmother.

"She's standing right next to you," I said when she put the tools on the tray. "She's wearing a pink suit and pearls."

"OK," the hygienist said more confidently, "I KNOW you're wrong now. Grandmother *never* wore anything like that!"

I just shrugged, and Grandmother smiled and waved.

A few days later, the hygienist gave me a call at home. She sounded a bit frightened.

"My husband and I looked under all the sinks in our home, and we found the box of things for my sister under one of them," she said. Her voice went up about half an octave when she added, "And my mother reminded me Grandmother wore the pink suit and pearls to my wedding, and she's buried in that outfit, too!"

"She says, 'Hi,' and she's very content," I told the woman. I also silently congratulated myself that I'd had the courage to own my abilities when Bonnie first asked me what I did. Because I had, Bonnie now had personal proof that the sixth sense is a very real, very provable thing.

Little Red Sports Car

Word of Grandmother's appearance spread quickly through the dental office, and on my next visit, the dentist himself asked if there was anyone trying to talk to *him*.

"That guy right there says you need more golf magazines in the waiting room," I told him, "And he said I'm supposed to ask you about the cigars and the little red sports car."

The dentist muttered under his breath, quickly looked to see if any of his employees were near, then shut the door to the exam room.

"That's RICHARD!" he said. He explained that this close friend and golf enthusiast had died recently, and had been buried with his clubs.

"Richard ALSO knows I haven't told anyone here about the cigars or the red sports car! No one knows I smoke, and everyone thinks I only have a hybrid! That's SO like him to try to stir things up!" We both laughed—and Richard was laughing, too. Obviously, our sense of humor remains intact when we journey to the other side. And, contrary to popular belief, dead men *do* tell tales.

Alien Dreams

It's fascinating to realize that the place where we spend a third of our life is, for all practical purposes, uncharted territory. In many cultures, the information and experiences we receive in the dream state are honored as important messages from a divine source. I have always received significant guidance and precognitive markers in my dreams, whether it's been Walt Disney barging in to redirect his company's marketing efforts; learning that I'm going to have a choice to live or die, or seeing a completed promotional spot that, when I produce it as I dreamed it, will win Emmy awards.

That's why a particularly vivid dream I had in November of 2002 is still as crystal clear as it was the night I experienced it.

I was standing in a room in the top floor of a skyscraper, and as I looked out the window, dozens of spaceships began decloaking. The discs covered the sky, and I intuitively knew the same scenario was being played out around the globe.

While the people of the Earth were choosing the meaning they were giving the alien visitors, the "mother ship" docked to the skyscraper where I stood. The extra-terrestrials aboard were of such an advanced technological culture they were able to merely reconfigure the molecular structure of the building, and their spaceship, to attach to each other, allowing their ship to become an extension of the skyscraper.

The being that appeared to be the main liaison to the humans was quite tall, with an elephantine head. I immediately thought of the Hindu God Ganesha. He was wearing a round flat hat and long robe, and both had the light green color of a copper patina. I realized his cloak and hat were actually elaborately woven living threads of infinite colors, but my human eyes weren't advanced enough to detect the highly evolved hues and patterns.

His species had morphed the trunk, allowing them to traverse galaxies and visit all forms of planets without requiring any auxiliary breathing apparatus. They could filter instantly and naturally any environment's atmosphere into a life-supporting substance through that trunk. I also realized what appeared to be huge black eyes were actually thin, round black filters that fit directly over their natural eyes, allowing them to adapt to the light quality of any solar system. There wasn't any feeling of a threat or implied control from the ET—rather a curious mix of disappointment and urgency.

It was then I realized that this visiting high council of ETs had "beamed" all the world leaders together, and assembled them in the huge area created by the docked spaceship.

"We had a deal," one of the ETs was saying to the humans. "You were supposed to tell your people that we were real before we arrived, so there wouldn't be fear." While this cosmic reckoning was underway, the Earth plunged into chaos under the shadows of the now visible UFOs.

In many cities and nations, people panicked. Feeling that the world was about to end anyway, some chose to loot stores, set buildings ablaze, rape, murder, destroy and play out unspeakably violent and terrible acts.

In other areas, special people stepped forward to calm and reassure the masses, emerging as spiritual leaders urging faith, hope, and peace.

Children in general were fascinated until they saw their parents recoil in fear—then they, too, began to scream and cry.

I awoke from the dream feeling unsettled, and knowing more would be revealed.

Within two weeks of that night, I happened to hear a report on NPR that the British Ministry of Defense was finally admitting it had covered up a UFO incident in 1980 in Rendlesham forest, a few miles from Bentwaters Royal Air Force Base. The personnel who witnessed the encounter were threatened into silence, the report revealed, and the public was deliberately misinformed about the incident.

Shortly after that, France also released previously sealed UFO reports, including some spectacular photographs.

I'm expecting the United States to follow suit shortly....

Dharma's Contribution

One of the reasons it's so much fun to consult with couples is you can get immediate confirmation. For instance, I'll say to the guy, "You're not very comfortable around other people, and frequently clam up at parties."

"No I *don't!*" he'll insist, and the woman chimes in, "Yes, you certainly do! You said two words all night at the Henderson's barbecue...."

But gently refocusing....

During a couple's session in my San Diego condo, I was deeply into the reading when I suddenly heard my cat come in through the kitty doors and do her "Xena Princess Warrior" howl. Unfortunately, that could mean only one thing—Dharma had just killed something for me, and was demanding I come accept her dead offering.

"Ah—just a minute, please," I said to the pair, and dashed into the kitchen. Sure enough, Dharma was posing proudly over a twisted lump of brown feathers. The valiant little bird's head was arched back at a horrid angle, his eyes were closed, and his wings were splayed across the white tiles.

Without even thinking, I scooped up the bird and held him in one hand with the other hand cupped over top. I silently prayed for him, and saw him as healthy, whole and...well...alive. Gently I blew a Reiki breath on him through the tiny space where my hands intersected, and continued to pray. That's when I realized the man and woman had followed me into the kitchen, and were watching intently.

I took a deep breath, and knew it was time. "Open the front door," I said.

"Wha...what?" the man asked.

"The front door," I answered, motioning to the foyer with my head. "Please open it."

They quickly moved to the door and the woman pulled it open. I stepped into the doorway, opened my hands, and the bird flew away. Both of their jaws dropped, and I saw real fear in their eyes as they stared at me. I knew I had to say something quickly to shift their energy—I was starting to feel their fear vibes that could have turned this into a "villagers with torches and pitchforks storming the house on the hill" scenario.

"Man," I said, shaking my head. "I have GOT to raise my rates!"

Thankfully, after a quick double take, they both started laughing. My comment was just SO over-the-top inappropriate, it completely knocked them for a loop. We resumed our reading and never said another word about what had just happened. Dharma was a bit miffed, though. She was looking forward to enjoying some shredded tweet....

He Was Healing by Helping

There's really no "safety net" for spiritual consulting the way I do it. I have no deck of cards to confirm what I'm feeling, no exacting degrees of one planet's orbit in the heavens to point to as the reason the client is doing whatever the heck the client is doing. I just put both the client and myself in white light, take a deep breath to alter how my brain works, and do a silent prayer to see the information the person needs to know.

I'm not a "unicorns and rainbows" kind of psychic, although there's certainly nothing WRONG with unicorns and rainbows. Rather, I work to get concrete, literal information that the person can immediately apply to her or his life. If something is vague, I insist the person not try to stretch to make it fit—I just "go back up" to get more specific details.

So it went the day a brilliant social worker booked an appointment to "test" me. The good-looking young man was deeply respected for the transformational work he did for abused children. Full of confidence and quite relaxed, he easily established rapport with kids and gently led them out of the darkness of their shame, fear, and hurt into the sunshine of a healing new start. Clients and colleagues alike loved him.

Sitting face to face at the start of our session, the man smiled and challenged me. "Tell me what the most traumatic event in my childhood was."

His verbal throwing down of the gauntlet didn't disturb me in the least. I welcome skeptics, and have always felt that until something is true for you personally, it's not really true. I did my silent prayer, took a breath, and immediately received a disturbing image.

"You were sexually abused," I told him.

His smile vanished, and was replaced by a look somewhere between scorn and anger. "That's RIDICULOUS!" he said through clenched teeth, color flushing his cheeks. "My father died when I was 12. THAT was the terrible thing!"

"Just a minute," I told him. I closed my eyes and forced myself to go to an even higher spiritual level. The pictures came quickly.

"The man who abused you had blond hair, and he was a bit chunky," I said.

"That is just SICK," the social worker responded, shaking his head. "If that would ever have happened, I would have remembered...."

"He was your little league coach. You wore red and white uniforms."

The man's protest died on his lips as every speck of color drained from his cheeks. I had cracked his cosmic egg, and I could see the painful memories he'd repressed for decades were flooding back. As he realized this truth, I silently asked for guidance in how to help him heal this reopened wound. The right words came, along with his tears.

This beautiful soul and wounded healer had taken his own terrifying experience and used it to become the perfect resource for other wounded youngsters. He truly understood their pain, and consistently, effectively helped them to release it. Now, it was *his* turn to reclaim the pieces of himself that had shattered and fallen away so he could survive. He continues to do his important work with kids.

The Letterman's Jacket

When traditional medicine can't help a patient, maybe someone who sees dead people is the person to call. So it was when a doctor from out of state contacted me.

"I've been working with a woman whose teenage son committed suicide a year and a half ago," the doctor said. "She's not responding to antidepressants or therapy, and she's totally shut herself off in her grief. She's so far out of it she can't even cry. She has other children she's just ignoring, and she hasn't moved on at all with her life. I was hoping you might be able to do something for her." I immediately agreed to try.

Normally, when I'm doing a session for a person, I've at least connected with them over the phone to get a read on their energy. For this woman, though, everything I did had to be without any input from her.

Sitting at my computer keyboard, I closed my eyes, took a deep breath, and just said, "OK, God, please make me an instrument of Your healing. Please show me what this woman needs to know."

Immediately, the pictures started coming. There was a very good-looking tall young man, with dark hair and glasses. He was jogging, with a light colored large dog by his side. The boy saw me watching him, then slowed down and started to talk to me. He said he was SO sorry about the grief he had caused his family and friends, and particularly, his mother. He regretted taking his life, and said he was temporarily not in his right mind—he was rather crazy over a girl. He was just trying to get her attention, not kill himself.

He said he was an athlete, and had multiple letters from his high school. Then he showed me his letter jacket hanging over the back of a chair in his bedroom, and said when his mom puts the jacket on, he can hug her.

While he was working through his regret at his actions, he was also watching over his family, and sending his love to them all. He wanted his mother to know he never really left her, and he wanted her to start being present for his younger siblings.

The whole time I was typing his message I was crying. There was SUCH love and devotion there, and this gorgeous young man's main concern was for the people he'd so suddenly left behind.

I re-read everything and debated whether to send the emotional message to the woman's e-mail address. Would she find comfort in what had been shown to me, or would she become even more upset? I wanted to do no harm, but there was definitely a chance this information would truly help her heal.

One little prop I use sometimes to help me decide a course of action is to visualize a traffic signal, and observe the color of the illuminated light. If it's red, I don't do it. If it's yellow, I proceed cautiously. But, this time, it was glowing green. I took a deep breath, and hit "Send." Then I sat there, staring at the computer screen. After about five minutes, I finally got up and started fixing dinner.

A few hours passed, and there was still no return message. I shut the computer off for the night.

Early the next morning I rolled out of bed and raced to the office. I turned on the computer, and went right to my e-mail. My heart stopped. There was a message from the woman. I closed my eyes, said a quick prayer, and hit "Open."

"I haven't stopped crying since I got your e-mail yesterday...." the note began. Uh-oh. Was she talking about *good* crying, or *bad* crying?

"Everything you said was true. The dog was Jason's collie, which was killed by a car the year before Jason died. He played three different sports. He was nuts about a girl in his class. And I DO feel him hugging me when I put on his letter jacket...." I had to stop reading to just sit back, wipe away my tears, and breathe a heart-felt prayer of thanks.

The woman thanked me profusely in her letter, and told me for the first time since Jason's death she could feel real emotion again. She knew her son hadn't just "disappeared," that he was still there for her in spirit. She could finally cry cleansing, healing tears.

A week later the woman's doctor contacted me again. "It's just amazing," he said. "She feels a reason to live again. She's started more traditional counseling, and is finally getting therapy to acknowledge and move through her grief without shutting down. You helped her get back into the world!"

Technically, it wasn't "me." I was just the earthly "cable hookup" for the information. But, it was wonderful to get confirmation that just doing what I do could help to rescue a mother from an emotional black hole. I was, and continue to be, so profoundly grateful.

Cat Tales

I've always connected with cats. Just ask my poor parents. Our house was usually filled with the pitter-patter of little paws, and the requisite sandpaper tongue prints in the butter. Circumstantial evidence, I'd always argue.

Fast-forward to 2002. Paul had crossed into the spirit realm the previous year. My heart still ached at the loss of the only man I ever truly loved, but my life was full with friends and my spiritual work. I stopped to get gas one evening when the "hunch" said, "Go to that PETCO at the end of the strip mall." I argued, saying, "I don't NEED anything from PETCO! I have plenty of cat food for Dharma (my exquisite tortoise shell)."

"GO TO THE PETCO!"

I've learned not to argue with the hunches. The minute I walked into the store, my eyes were pulled to a cage against the wall. Three rescued coal-black kittens huddled together on a blanket. Suddenly, the long-haired one stood up, locked eyes with me, and started to crawl up the metal wire of the cage to get to me. That's how I found Minerva McGonagall, whom I named after the Gryffindor Headmistress from the *Harry Potter* books. She was the wonderful character who turned into a cat to spy on her students. Minerva is also the Roman goddess of wisdom, healing, and war.

While Dharma was not pleased—she insisted we did not NEED a pet—Minnie settled into the household routine quickly. Normally before I go to sleep, I do a quick affirmation and put myself, the room, and the entire house in white light. Unfortunately, I apparently forgot this little ritual one night right after I adopted Minerva, because I was attacked by two demonic beings in my "dream." It was that bewildering state where you're asleep, but not really asleep, and I was frantically trying to summon up the strength to banish the evil things, raise the energy in the room, and rededicate the room back to God.

Suddenly I felt a hand on my shoulder, and a surge of strength poured into me. I had the power to get rid of the demons, and immediately after they vanished, I forced myself literally to wake up. I was shocked, AND relieved, to find Minerva on my pillow, gazing directly into my eyes, with her paw on my shoulder. She's really not fooling ANYONE with that cat suit she's wearing!

Spinning Wheels

For several months I'd been feeling like I'd fallen into a rut. I love to write (double Gemini in the third house, Pisces rising), and that will always be an important part of my professional life, but I wondered if I was dedicating enough time to my spiritual work. The day after Christmas I was upstairs in my condo with my cats when I suddenly heard a "Whirrrrrrr" coming from the living room.

I cautiously ventured downstairs and turned on the light. Somehow, a Lego remote-controlled car Paul had built the year before he died had fallen off the coffee table, landed on its side, and turned itself on (?). Its little wheels were spinning away, generating that loud whirring noise.

"OoooKAY, Honey," I laughed, "I get the message!" That, combined with a few deceased friends coming to yell at me several days later in a mediumship demonstration by the incredible Hollister Rand, had all the subtlety of a train crashing through a plate glass window.

Seeing the handwriting on the wall or, in this case, the toy wheels spinning on the car, I knew it was time to create my "Happy Medium" Web site (happymedium.us), and step into my destiny.

"Cleaning the Room" From a Continent Away

When my beautiful niece Katie, my younger brother's middle daughter, graduated from high school and embarked on her college career, I was thrilled for her. She was leaving the cloistered rural life in Emmaus, Pennsylvania, for the halls of American University in Washington, D.C. to study communications and public relations. Katie is brilliant, and I knew she'd do great in a competitive, fast-paced environment.

The sweet little country gal was getting dropkicked into a whole different world, though, and there were bound to be some necessary adjustments.

Sure enough, a few days into Katie's first term, I got a call from my mom. "Katie's having some challenges with her roommate," Mom said. "Apparently she's not as friendly and easy-going as Katie, and it's been tough for her."

With Pisces rising and five planets in Cancer, of COURSE I wanted to rush right in and fix everything. No one was going to be mean to my sweet niece!

Now, if you only think of dowsing as weathered old men walking around with a willow branch to find where to dig a well, you might want to take notes.

Raymon Grace, a genuine Appalachian mountain man, opened my eyes to all the incredible things dowsing with either rods or a pendulum can do. I have the deepest respect for Raymon's work because he's totally coming from the heart, and genuinely wants to be of service. He's also documented his results, proving after his dowsing sessions such things as arsenic disappearing from wells, and even the crime rate going way down in a Canadian town.

There's no real magic to dowsing. It's merely a powerful tool for focusing your energy so you can mindfully concentrate on shifting people, places or things from negative to positive, or dark to light. He explains it all in detail on his Web site at www.RaymonGrace.com.

I had just taken a workshop with him, and decided to try pendulum dowsing to clear Katie's dorm room of negative energies. I tied a ring on a string, cut the string to about a seven-inch length, and sat down at the kitchen table. Holding the string between my thumb and index finger, I put myself in white light first, and simply asked God to show me a "Yes."

Without me moving my hand, the ring slowly started swinging towards and away from me. I asked to see a "No," and the ring stopped then ever so slowly began swinging from left to right. "Please show me a 'working on it,'" I said next, and the ring stopped again, and then started going in a counter-clockwise circular path. "And please show me an 'it is done,'" I finished, and the ring stopped again then started swinging in a clockwise direction. Great. We were calibrated.

"Thank you, Spirit. Now, is it appropriate for me to try to heal the energies in Katie's dorm room?" Again without me moving my hand at all, the ring slowly started swinging to and fro, indicating a "Yes" from Spirit.

"Thank you. Then I ask that all negative energies in and around Katie's college dorm room be transmuted into kindness, compassion, patience and friendship," I said aloud. As I continued specifying the positive vibes I wanted for her, the ring began spinning in a HUGE counter-clockwise circle, picking up speed. Even after I was done affirming the shift I desired to manifest, the ring continued spinning for maybe another 90 seconds. Gradually it slowed, and then came to a complete stop. I continued to watch, with my hand remaining motionless, as the ring then began to make a clockwise rotation, spinning around a few more times before coming back to a complete rest, indicating the shift was done.

"Thank you!" I said, pleased at the dramatic dance of the ring on a string. And that was that.

A few days later, mom called again. "It's just amazing," she said. "Shortly after we spoke, Katie and her roommate just seemed to be fine. There's no more unpleasantness. They've even become friends!"

"Wow, that's great news!" I said. "Gee, I wonder what happened to change everything for them?"

"Whatever it was, it's wonderful," mom said. "Katie just seemed to work it out."

Yeaaa, Katie!

Chapter 14

Back to the Mountains!

While I just loved Southern California, toward the end of 2004 I was getting very strong messages in dreams and visions that I was going to be moving soon. While it was sad to be leaving the beautiful state Paul and I had shared for a decade, I also realized it was time to get on with my life. California had been Paul's home. I had to find mine.

There were two places I felt calling to me—Santa Fe, with its Southwestern magic and powerful spiritual vibe, and the Asheville, North Carolina area. Asheville is where I ended my two-year spiritual quest back in my 20s, and the lush green forests and breath-taking mountain views had remained in my heart and mind.

Both areas had their unique charm and spiritual promise, and after a few weeks of waiting for divine guidance, I felt I was being "pushed" back to the East coast. Still, I continued to ask for confirmation I'd made the correct decision, and I didn't have long to wait. While an end-unit condo identical to mine and just across the street had been on the market for months, I found my buyer 15 minutes after I put out my realtor's "For Sale" sign. The realtor had suggested a $20,000 window in my asking price, and this buyer offered the full amount. Sold!

The second sign came within the week. I picked a book off a shelf, and a postcard fell out. I picked the card up to read it, and was shocked—well, just a little bit surprised, maybe—to see it was addressed to me at my old Asheville apartment. I had received it 25 years earlier, tucked it in that book, and forgotten about it for a quarter of a century.

Still another indicator I was going in the right direction came while I was sitting in the San Diego condo, clicking through MLS listings for Asheville, 3,000 miles away. One particular home jumped through the screen at me, and it seemed perfect. An old friend from Asheville—who just happens to be a psychology professor -- recommended a great realtor, and I arranged to fly to the city, meet her, and have her show me some potential homes. As we were driving up to the one I found, I got chills. Then when she opened the lock box, retrieved the house key, unlocked the door and we walked inside, I began to cry. I knew this was my new place.

The realtor put in my offer, which was immediately accepted, and the sale progressed quickly. Several dear friends helped me pack up the San Diego condo, and I tearfully watched as movers loaded my life into a huge semi. Both cats got to make the cross-country journey in carry-on cages tucked under airplane seats, and they have *not* let me forget it. I was saying good-bye to Paul, and opening the book on the next chapter of my life.

Spirited Welcoming Committee

The first day in my new mountain home was a dream. The previous owner had turned the old two-car garage into a great room, with cedar paneling, huge picture windows, and a high ceiling. Then, he had built a three-car garage onto the side of the house to hold his vintage automobiles.

Both cats, who had just endured that cross-country flight in small pet carriers, raced through the empty rooms, sniffing, staring through the many windows, stalking the birds on a patio railing from behind the sliding glass door, and angling for the warmest sunny spots on the carpets.

Disregarding what my new neighbors might think, I smudged the inside and outside of my new home, and dedicated it back to the Earth, and the Cherokee. I declared it as a sacred space to heal the healers and teach the teachers.

Since the furniture wouldn't be arriving for at least another week, I slept that first night on a futon in front of the fireplace. I just drifted off when I was startled awake by a strong presence. I opened my eyes, and a huge light blue orb, about four feet in diameter, was floating above me.

I gasped—it was so energetically powerful, yet loving and gentle. I felt it was either the spirit of the Cherokee and the mountains, or a friendly ET, welcoming me home. Or, perhaps it was one and the same. I gave the sphere my deepest gratitude, and fell into a wonderful, peaceful sleep.

Cosmic Connections

After I returned to the ancient mountains of Western North Carolina, I was contacted by one of the first participants in the college intern program I started at WLOS-TV. She was now a divorced mom of two, and a freelance writer. We met for lunch and had a delightful time catching up. She wondered if I was still doing intuitive work, and then asked me to take a "look" at her son and daughter, who were both in elementary school at that time of the day.

I intuitively connected first with her daughter, and gave my friend information she immediately confirmed. Then I mentally linked up with her autistic son.

As is the case with most autistic people, I immediately saw he was brilliant and had many talents, including phenomenal musical ability. I spent more time in his energy, sharing additional details and offering some ideas about opportunities coming up for the boy.

Later that afternoon, my friend picked up her kids at the end of the school day.

"I had lunch with someone I used to work with years ago," she started to tell them.

"MOM!" her son exclaimed. "THAT LADY WAS LOOKING AT ME!"

From miles away, this sensitive young man had felt me merging with his energy, or, in quantum physics parlance, "doing an entanglement on the Universal Field."

Be mindful of what you're thinking about someone! On some level, they will "know" you're tapping into them.

Stopping on a Dime

For a few weeks in August of 2006, I had the vague feeling I was going to be in a car crash. Each time I clairaudiently heard the sensation of crunching metal I would dissolve it into light, working to shift the energies and prevent the premonition from coming into reality.

Then, one day on a whim, I decided to take my rescued black Labrador Bear to his favorite lake for a walk. I loaded him into the back of my 2005 Subaru Forester and started driving south. Because of the premonition, I was particularly cautious behind the wheel, and used "'industrial strength white light" constantly.

As we approached an intersection where I had a green light, I slowed down to allow an oncoming truck to make a left, and cross directly in front of my lane of traffic. Unfortunately, a kid in a beat-up 1989 rusty blue Thunderbird who was right behind the truck stomped on the gas to also race through the light illegally—I had the right of way. I braced for impact and turned my car to the left, hoping to minimize the damage. No such luck.

Because the kid was gunning it, he totaled his car, and mangled my hood and right front end. Metal screamed, glass exploded, and the cars skidded to a stop in the center of the busy intersection. Bear, who was shaking like a leaf, immediately put both front paws on the console and leaned all 106 pounds against me. He was going to protect me, with no concern for his own safety.

A young cop arrived quickly, and interviewed me while a wad of tobacco he'd been chewing remained securely tucked under his lower lip. He punctuated his questions with an occasional spit into his Coke can. Bottom line, the kid in the Ford was clearly at fault and got tagged with a ticket. My car was drivable, and Bear and I were bruised and shaken but not seriously injured. Most thankfully, the accident I felt coming had happened, and although it was painful and caused great inconvenience, it wasn't catastrophic.

A few weeks later, while my car remained in a body shop for extensive repair, and both Bear and I continued to need chiropractic treatments, I went into a bit of a funk about the whole experience. Why had this happened? Was this just a random thing, an isolated, insignificant event in the cosmos that caused pointless suffering? I prayed and asked God for some insight.

Immediately, a voice said, "Go to the dresser." I walked into my bedroom and went to stand in front of the dresser. "Pick two coins," I heard next. Taking a deep breath, I reached into the coin dish on the dresser and picked out two dimes. With no additional directions being offered, I took a closer look at the two coins, and blinked hard.

The date on one of them was 2005, the year of my car. The date on the other? 1989, the year of the other driver's Ford.

Well, OK, but that could have just been a coincidence. One by one, I took every other coin out of the dish—about two dozen in all—and checked the dates on each one. There was not another 2005 or 1989 in the bunch.

I felt I had just received cosmic confirmation that the crash was NOT random. Even though it was hard for me to understand it at the time, there was a divine order and purpose in the unpleasant experience. There was no doubt it would eventually be revealed to me. I took comfort in the knowing.

The Cow Whisperer

When the co-editor/publisher of Western North Carolina Woman magazine celebrated her 60th birthday, I volunteered to help coordinate the food part of the festivities. (All you readers with a lot of planets in Cancer will certainly understand why I've become the "unofficial caterer" for all my friends' gatherings!) A big group of Sandi's friends transformed a popular yoga studio into a dance floor and buffet, and we all had a blast.

As I was enjoying the music, Sandi's daughter came up and introduced herself.

"I understand you're an animal communicator," Julie said.

"Yes," I answered.

"My husband and I have a cow named Priscilla on our farm, and she's getting aggressive toward the other animals, and our children," Julie explained. "We don't want to get rid of her, but we can't have her threatening everything, either. Can you find out what's wrong?"

There's certainly no trick to accurate animal communication; just move your consciousness from your head, where everything is analytical, and into your heart, where it's all feeling and love. From that place of non-judgment and connection, you can gently yet powerfully link up with animals, children, plants, really just about anything.

"Sure," I told Julie. "Just a minute while I go up and check."

"Going up" is my terminology for simply taking a deep breath, and entering into a prayer state. I push my awareness up into a higher state of Universal Consciousness, where we're all connected. While I prefer to approach it from a spiritual base, the process is simply shifting into an alpha brain wave state, and then "feeling" your intent to connect with a specific person, place, or thing.

Despite the laughter, dancing and loud conversations happening all around us, I was immediately able to connect with the cow and "talk" with Priscilla. The information I got was way out there, but I've learned through the decades not to edit or judge.

"OK, Julie," I said, "The problem is you're treating her like a regular cow, and she's actually royalty. Her name isn't 'Priscilla,' it's 'Anastasia.' You need to treat her with great deference—she has to be the first animal greeted and fed when you go to the barn, and it wouldn't hurt if you'd even genuflect a bit."

At this point BOTH Julie and I were laughing, but she promised she'd try at least a few of my bizarre suggestions. A day or two later, Sandi relayed that Julie and her husband had indeed started treating the cow as I suggested, and Priscilla had completely changed her attitude.

First of all, they began calling her "Czarina," which she seemed to love. She relished getting her meal before any of the other animals, and happily responded to the sometimes exaggerated attention the whole family showered upon her.

Julie was pleased with the dramatic transformation in the cow, but her logical side struggled to understand why it was happening. On a whim, she decided to Google more information about The-Cow-Formerly-Known-as-Priscilla, and almost fell off her chair. By tracing the cow's breeding stock, she learned it was descended from a Royal Jersey bull that had been in the Russian court of Czar Alexander II. Mystery solved!

Releasing Dominique

The beautiful woman arrived for her reading on the brink of tears. After greeting her and getting her comfortably settled, I put both of us in the white light of Universal Consciousness and gently asked her how I could help her.

"It's my son," Selina DeLangre explained. He was 28, and was born so crippled with cerebral palsy and cystic fibrosis his doctors said he wouldn't live to his teens. He had never been able to utter a word, walk, or control any of his movements.

"He's starting to have seizures frequently, and I just don't know what to do for him. Can you help me?"

Selina's grief tinged with guilt tore at my heart, and I surrounded myself with extra white light to be able to avoid being drawn into her tortured emotional state. Compassion is fine, but an effective intuitive counselor has to have good energetic boundaries. The woman needed solid information, not just someone to cry with her.

I took a deep breath, asked God to show me what the woman needed to know, and then began to relay the information I received immediately.

"First of all," I told her, "Your son isn't 'broken,' so he doesn't need to be fixed. He's beautiful and perfect, just the way he is." Selina sat back and looked at me, hard.

"He's stayed here an extra 18 years waiting for you to realize that, and to release your guilt that somehow, his physical condition is your 'fault.' It's not! It's what he signed up to experience this lifetime."

Now the woman's jaw dropped, but she continued to hang on my every word. I took another deep breath to stay in a high Alpha state, out of my own ego, and in Christ Consciousness for Divine guidance.

"After you release your own guilt and see the perfection in this beautiful soul, he wants you to release him to the Light, too. He's forcing his body to keep functioning until you come into that awareness, even though it's taking quite a toll on him."

Now Selina was sobbing into a handful of tissues. I could see the energy shifting around her, though, and knew she understood this tough but true message. Gently, I explained to her what I had done when my husband was nearing his final time. I bought a bunch of little crystal prisms, the kind you hang in a window. He held a crystal for each of his close friends and family members, blessing it with everything he wanted for that person, and then put each in a box marked with the person's name. After Paul's death I distributed them. Now we all have rainbows every day that Paul made for us.

The woman loved that idea, and left my office with a new sense of peace and purpose. Our session was Thursday. On Friday, Selina visited a local gift shop and bought a number of crystals. Then, on Saturday, she went to her son's bedside.

She told the young man how much she loved him, and how beautiful and perfect he was. She told him she realized now he didn't need to be fixed, because he wasn't broken. She thanked him for his great personal sacrifice to stay in a failing physical form until she could finally understand these truths, and know that she had nothing about which to feel guilty. As Selina spoke to her son, even though he couldn't verbally respond, he beamed at her and made happy vocalizations.

Then, she told him about the crystals, and how he could make rainbows for her, his sisters, and other family and friends. One by one, Selina pressed the crystals into his hand, telling him for whom each crystal was. He smiled, and laughed, and swung his head from side to side, obviously quite happy.

After he held the last crystal, the woman told her son he was perfect, she loved him, she was so grateful to him, and she released him when he was ready to go. Selina bent over him to kiss him, and right then, as she held him, that beautiful boy took his last breath.

Pam's Class Act

My sister-in-law Pam Espinosa not only gave me her wonderful brother when she introduced us at Disneyland—she gave me her friendship, which remains an important and deeply cherished part of my life. When we first met in the Public Relations department at Disneyland back in 1991, we were miles apart as far as our intuitive experiences. I pretty much lived in the spiritual realm, while Pam was more skeptical. Through the years, though, she continued to have more and more experiences that crossed over into my area, and she's come full-circle as far as her belief in our ability to connect with people on the other side.

She's currently a fifth grade teacher in the Seattle area. Recently she gave her students a writing assignment, and worked at her desk while the class silently wrote on their tablets. Suddenly, Pam felt a cold breeze come over her legs. She knew, both from things I'd shared with her and some popular movies, most notably *The Sixth Sense*, that an entity in spirit had just approached her. She forced herself to continue working—she didn't want to react dramatically and possibly scare a roomful of 10-year-olds.

While Pam managed to maintain her composure, she noticed two little girls get up from their seats and approach her desk.

"Ms. Espinosa," one of them said earnestly, "Is there a ghost in our classroom?"

Pam gulped, but displayed no outward reaction.

"Now why would you ask that?" she said to the girls.

"Because we felt a cold breeze pass between us," the other little girl answered. "Doesn't that mean there's a ghost walking by?"

"Well, yes it DOES," Pam said calmly. "But have you both finished your writing assignment yet?"

"No, Ms. Espinosa," the girls chorused in unison, then trooped back to their seats.

That, by the way, was the perfect reaction. While Pam validated the girls' experience, she let them know that it certainly wasn't anything to get frightened or flustered about. It was perfectly normal, and didn't mean the girls could abandon their responsibilities. When she shared the story with me, I gave her a gold star.

Quite an Impression

When Paul and I married, an antique table he'd found at a flea market became the centerpiece of our kitchen. It was wobbly but magnificent, with fine craftsmanship, and an elegant dark stain. For years I sat at that table, and after Paul's death it became even more precious to me for the happy memories it held. I decided to haul it cross-country with me when I left San Diego to return to the mountains of Western North Carolina.

About six months after I'd been back in North Carolina, I was sitting at that table reading the paper and having breakfast, as I always did. However, this day was different. I finished the paper and folded it up, then stopped. There, at the place I'd sat for 16 years, was a name carved into the surface of the table and filled in with black ink. **J-i-m**. I thought someone must have broken in and carved it!

My neighbor, a woodworker, loaned me some cleaning compound to remove the letters. They didn't budge. He came over to take a look, and said, "That's been covered with varnish. That name has been there a long time." The "**J-i-m**" was nearly two inches high—there was NO way I could have missed seeing it for the past decade and a half.

Dear reader, you might recall that a huge part of my North Carolina experience from 1979—83 revolved around the United Research Light Center, and its founder, Jim Goure. He's the one who originally convinced me to move to North Carolina to be the resident psychic at the Light Center.

Every time I've tried to "see" psychically which Jim decided to leave his mark, I come up blank. I always have to laugh, though, every time I see that name. I know the answer will be clear when the time is right. The odds of it just "showing up" right now, as I'm back here in the Carolina mountains, is just too—fantastic, as Jim would say.

Reiki and Deeksha

Through a series of happy coincidences and synchronicities, I ended up becoming a Deeksha Blessing Giver the day the founder of this particular form of energy medicine fast-tracked the process for the world.

Although Deeksha started in India with spiritual teachers Sri Bhagavan and Sri Padmavathi Amma, it is not aligned with any religion or culture. There are over 15 million practitioners worldwide as this book goes to press.

Deeksha is the transference of spiritual energy into the neocortex of the brain through the Oneness Blessing Giver placing his or her hands directly on the receiver's head. The purpose of Deeksha is to awaken consciousness, and instill feelings of peace, calmness, and connectedness to all of creation.

Previously people who wanted to bestow the Oneness Blessing (as Deeksha is also known) to others, had to attend a 21-day class in India. To make the training more palatable to Westerners, it eventually morphed into a weeklong class in Fiji. Then, the first week of December 2009, Sri Bhagavan turned the old Deeksha paradigm on its spiritual ear.

The world's need for more Deeksha Givers mandated that the process be streamlined even further, he decreed, and anyone who had ever attended the two-day Oneness Blessing Weekend seminar could be initiated as Blessing Givers by dedicated trainers.

At that time there were only 14 certified trainers in the nation, and—happy coincidence!—two of them lived in Asheville and were dear friends of mine. Kathi and Sheldon Butler immediately scheduled an initiation session at their home, and nearly a dozen of us who previously attended weekend seminars became Blessing Givers that very day.

The experience was sacred, profound, joyful, and humbling. As Kathi's hands rested on my head during my initiation, chills rushed up my spine, and lights exploded in front of my eyes. I felt the presence of hundreds—maybe thousands—of beings in spirit joining us in the Butler's cozy family room. I silently rededicated myself to being of service, and remembered the words of the psychic who told me when I was 17 that I was going to be one of the leaders in raising world consciousness. The experience this time, as it did when I was a teen, left me humbled, overwhelmed, and deeply honored and grateful to the opportunity to use what I had to help others. More chills.

After we were each initiated, we circulated among members of our little group, trading off giving and receiving the Deeksha blessings. It was a precious jewel of a day.

Since that evening, I've shared Deeksha blessings with many people, and I've become quite clear on the energetic difference between Deeksha and Reiki. I mentioned Reiki earlier in the book, and shared the article I wrote about pioneering American Reiki Master Virginia Samdahl. Reiki just recently received a huge push into mainstream consciousness when Dr. Oz, the renowned cardiac surgeon who's been a frequent guest on Oprah, endorsed it on his popular TV show. Reiki Master and author Pamela Miles, who has worked with Dr. Oz during surgeries, demonstrated Reiki for the television audience.

With Reiki healing, the practitioner becomes the hollow bone through which universal healing energy flows. The healer's hands can be either directly on or just inches above the receiver, and there are several specific places on the receiver's body where the healer sends the energy. Distance Reiki can be directed to the intended receiver from a completely different location, or even a different time. By that, I mean a Reiki healer can send Reiki into a person's past to help them heal a hurt from childhood, or even in utero. Reiki can be sent to a future event, too, like an upcoming surgery.

The Reiki healer functions like jumper cables, sending Universal life energy into the receiver for the receiver to use as they wish. Reiki energy goes to the receiver's body, mind, and spirit, wherever it is most needed.

Deeksha, however, is channeling energy with a different intent. Deeksha is bestowed specifically to raise the receiver's consciousness, kind of like rewiring the brain to a higher frequency, and propelling him or her into a higher state of awareness and being. It helps the receiver be much more mindful of every aspect of his or her life, and achieve a sense of interconnectedness to everyone and everything on the planet. The receiver usually achieves an emotional, mental and spiritual sense of calmness. This elevated consciousness can easily *lead* to physical healing, but that's not the intended focus.

Unlike a Reiki session, in which practitioners usually lay their lands on several parts of the receiver's body, a Oneness Blessing Giver is instructed to place both hands only on the receiver's head. Each Reiki hand position can last up to eight minutes, while Deeksha is a transfer lasting from 20 seconds to a minute or two. The Oneness Blessing can also be sent remotely.

Both Reiki and Deeksha draw on Universal Life force, which flows through the practitioner into the receiver.

I personally feel both are powerful, sacred, and effective ways to share energy. It is an honor to be a channel for Reiki *and* Deeksha.

"If it Was Necessary...."

Spiritsong is a phenomenally talented astrologer and energy healer in Asheville. She is also a dear friend.

Because I'm so darned sensitive to other people's vibes, I'm very particular about the person I choose to work on me. Whether it's a dentist, medical doctor, massage therapist or even a hair stylist—if a person is tense, angry, hurried or judgmental, I feel it. I automatically put up a shield to deflect his or her spiky energy, and shut myself off from getting the real benefit of the treatment.

Spiritsong, who surrounds her clients in heart-felt compassion and a sincere desire to serve, is one of the main practitioners I turn to when I'm feeling out of sorts.

On this particular afternoon, Spiritsong had me lie on her treatment table in her home office and covered me with a sheet. As I closed my eyes, I could smell a luscious bouquet of her healing essential oils envelop me—lavender, sandalwood, geranium, cinnamon—it was so calming. She also placed a gentle instrumental arrangement on her CD player. We were ready to begin.

Spiritsong began with a brief prayer asking for assistance and guidance from the angelic realm, then began looking for blocks in my energy. She moved her hands in the air a few inches away from my body, checking for any areas that felt "hot" or "cold."

As she was working in my auric field, I was silently praying to release all negative thoughts, emotions, and physical blocks that might be thwarting my efforts to be in balance on physical, mental, and spiritual levels.

Suddenly I felt the sensation of being pulled backwards into a portal; it was kind of like falling through a hole in time and space. Instantly I saw myself standing in a field in ancient Roman-occupied Greece. I intuitively knew I was an Essene mystic. Facing me in my vision was a Roman Centurion, and I recognized him as my modern-day father. As I watched the vision, the Centurion pulled his broadsword out of its sheath and stabbed me in my left side, piercing my heart and killing me instantly.

While my physical body from that lifetime crumbled to the ground, my spiritual body rose up, and blessed the soldier who had just delivered me to the other side. The Centurion was able to actually see my "ghost," and fell to his knees in equal measures of terror and regret that he had just killed a woman who was now forgiving him.

I was aware of a powerful disembodied male voice asking me, "Would you do it again?" I knew he meant, would I give my life for my spiritual beliefs?

Without hesitation, I silently affirmed, "If it was necessary."

The graphic blast from the past didn't need a psychic to interpret it—it just confirmed that I picked a father this lifetime who would constantly challenge my beliefs because of what I embraced as truth. All the decades of his condescension and ridiculing of my spiritual convictions and experiences—all of that dismissive behavior, was exactly what I signed up for—again.

It had forced me to take a stand, to release the assumption that I had to make everyone or *any*one else happy with my beliefs. I needed to develop that clear connection to God, to feel that divine sense of oneness, and to live my life according to the spiritual knowing I receive from a Higher Authority. Even the threat of death wasn't strong enough to make me renounce the Christ Conscious state of being that defined my path this lifetime. I could clearly see how important my father had been in helping me become and stay strong in my spiritual beliefs.

While this miraculous revelation was happening on a spiritual level, what transpired on the physical was just as dramatic.

At the moment the Centurion drove his blade into my heart, a wave of energy shot off my body and zapped across the room, literally knocking out Spiritsong's CD player.

She patiently waited until my consciousness returned to the present day and time, then invited me to share my experience. We both realized my connecting the dots about why my dad had been so tough on me about my beliefs represented a milestone in my spiritual growth. Thankfully we were also able to heal Spiritsong's CD player—she just had to turn it back on.

Jeffrey (Exit Stage Right)

Jeffrey, my bratty little brother, grew into an exceptional dad to four exceptional kids, and a brilliant attorney. While we actively plotted to kill each other when we were young, we became quite close by the time we entered our teens. He was the one person in my family who understood and encouraged my spiritual journey, and through the years we had many rich discussions sharing our different perspectives on theology, reality, intuitive ability, humor and just about everything else.

Shortly after I moved back to the East Coast, he and his wife came down from Emmaus, Pennsylvania, to spend several days with me in my new home. We had a blast. I took them for an afternoon tour of the fabled Biltmore Estate. We ate at my favorite restaurants. He loved his ride on the Smoky Mountain Parkway, and we had several hours of those great conversations we'd relished for decades. He even wanted the old refrigerator I had sitting in the garage—so I let him load it in his van. It was a fantastic visit, and it turned out to be the last time I saw him alive.

In April 2008, I turned off my cell phone to attend a business networking luncheon. As I was walking out to my car after the event, I turned the phone back on and saw I had a message.

"Jonna Rae, call me right away," my dad's voice commanded. I was concerned at his tone, and immediately dialed the number. I got his voice mail, so I called Jeff's number, and got his voice mail, too.

"Hey, Dude," I said, "I just got a call from Dad, and it doesn't sound good. Have you heard anything? Is Mom OK? Please call me as soon as you can."

Our mother had been seriously ill for several years, and Jeff and I had frequently shared our concerns about her failing health. In fact, when he and I had a brief falling out a few years earlier, I got him to break the icy silence by telling him I didn't want the next time I saw him to be at a funeral. He knew I was referring to Mom's shaky grasp on life, and he called immediately. We patched up our misunderstanding and were as close as ever.

But back to that day in April.... When I couldn't get Jeff, I left a message for my older brother in Lancaster, Pennsylvania. I tried to tune in and psychically see what was going on, but I was too worried to get a clear picture. Ideally, when I'm working to tune into someone or something on an intuitive level, I'll first become calm and take a few deep breaths to get into proper spiritual alignment. Then, instantly, I'll be able to tap into the source and receive accurate information. When I'm worried, like I was that day, it's difficult for me to get a clear connection.

Finally my dad called back.

"It's Jeffrey," he said, his voice breaking. "He's had a brain aneurysm. He's in a coma."

I tearfully asked him to keep me posted, then hung up the phone and started to pray through my sobs.

"Lord, make me an instrument of Thy healing and Thy love," I said. "Let me be of service!" As I sat on the couch, crying my heart out, I suddenly got a crystal clear vision of Jeff. He was standing in front of me, wearing a robe of sparkling white. Waves of rainbows emanated from his body, and his expression was pure love and grace. He was so peaceful, focused, and magnificent.

"Oh, Jeff!" I sobbed. "You're leaving, aren't you?"

He didn't speak words to answer me, but rather sent me his thoughts as he stood in a vortex of light and love.

He *was* getting ready to go, he confirmed.

"Should I head to Pennsylvania?" I asked through my tears.

"No," he answered silently. "Wait for my funeral." Then he showed me exactly where in his brain the bleed was. He asked me to be the spiritual godmother to his kids, because he knew there would be a day when they would have questions about the spiritual realm he and I discussed so passionately, and frequently. He wanted me to promise to be there to give them loving, accurate answers. Then it was time for him to go.

He didn't reach out his arms to embrace me, and I understood there was something about the dimension where he was while his body was in a coma that prevented that kind of energetic connection. Instead, he gently bent down slightly to touch his forehead to mine in the typical Buddhist greeting—and in a brilliant flash of light, he was gone.

First I collapsed in a sobbing heap on the floor, and then I thanked God for the opportunity to have had that sacred meeting. As soon as I could stand, I made my way to my desk and fell into the chair. I reached for my phone, and was so grateful to get my spiritual mentor immediately.

"Jeni," I sobbed, "My little brother is dying. My heart is just breaking!"

"We'll pray for him, and send Reiki to him," she said soothingly. Dr. Rev. Jeni Prigmore and her husband, Dr. Rev. Rick Prigmore, founded the Universal Brotherhood Movement, a non-denominational church that requires its ministers to take a vow to be of service to mankind. They are some of the sweetest, most loving and gentle souls I've ever known, and I was so grateful to have met them back in 1984, when they ordained me. Not only did I receive the mantle of the Universal Brotherhood, I received their friendship, which has been such a gift through the decades.

While Jeni and I prayed and cried together, my cat, Dharma, jumped up on the desk. She walked right up to me and pressed her furry head against my forehead, just as Jeff had done. I cried harder.

As the days unfolded, it became an emotional roller coaster. Jeff was kept in a coma to try to minimize the stress to his brain and body. His wife is a trauma nurse and nursing professor, so she could constantly monitor his care, work closely with his medical team, and explain to the rest of us what was happening. My older brother Dave also kept in close touch with Jeff's doctors, and he and I cried together during our frequent calls. It's so sad when a parent's life starts inching away, though it's not entirely unexpected. But a brother? A YOUNGER brother? We couldn't wrap our heads or hearts around the tragedy that was playing out.

While the medical team worked non-stop to try and find the source of the bleed in Jeff's brain, keep his body temperature low and reduce stress to his brain and body, the days turned into weeks. One by one, his four children were able to come back from the three states where they worked or went to school.

Even though Jeff stayed in a coma, he was able to respond to some commands. One daughter could say, "Squeeze my hand, Dad," and he would. At one point he opened his eyes, and another daughter said, "I think he can hear us!" He slightly nodded his head. We were all thrilled—it looked like he was defying all odds, and regaining consciousness.

During this apparently miraculous recovery, his ventilator was taken out at one point and his wife and kids were helping him sit up. I was SO praying my vision had been wrong. But, the day after still more wonderful improvements, he had a SECOND brain bleed, completely removed from the first. The doctors couldn't get over how bizarre it was to have a patient have two completely separate bleeds within days of each other.

Jeffrey was following through with his plan, but for 17 days after he had that first aneurysm, he gave his family and friends a chance to have closure. His wife and kids got to say what they wanted to say, and he squeezed their hands in a final gesture of love and connection. And then, gracefully, he crossed into the spirit world.

It was my dad who called with the news that Jeff was really gone. As I hung up the phone, I distinctly heard Jeff's teasing voice say, "Well, that's ONE less lawyer in the world!" It was so typical of his bizarre sense of humor that I laughed through the tears.

When I was talking with a friend about this entire sacred passage, he said, "How the heck can you find something positive in any of this?"

I guess I always force myself to search for a glimmer of something positive because on some level, I know there really *isn't* "death" as we might think of it—the complete cessation of any consciousness or connection. It certainly doesn't make it hurt any less, but it keeps me putting one foot in front of the other.

I see things that shake me to the core, but again, I push myself to find the beauty, the irony, the joke or the bigger reason for it, whatever the situation is. Does this make me truly different or any better than other people? Of course not. Everyone has the same capacity to traverse myriad dimensions simultaneously. There's a cost, though, and it includes the isolation I frequently feel when I don't have lots of people with whom I can so openly share my own experiences.

That's why Jeff's crossing, even though I "intellectually and spiritually" know he's still here, is so, so, so heartbreaking. It's like In *Star Wars*, when Obi-Wan Kenobi felt a "break in the force" when Vader's Death Star destroyed Princess Leia's home world of Alderaan. While I ache at the loss, I deeply know, and feel, and even see, that Jeff and Paul are both always close by.

Jeff Gets His Spirit Legs

Shortly after Jeff's death, I started to do a reading for my photographer friend Max Poppers at his home. I had no sooner done my initial prayer than a deafening crack came from the left side of the ceiling, sounding for all the world like a wooden bat driving into the plaster, but leaving no mark. We both jumped.

I took a deep breath and said, "Jeff, that was WAY over the top."

Max, who knew my brother had recently died, smiled and patted my hand.

"OK, let's try this again," I said. I closed my eyes and took another deep breath, then started my silent prayer again. THIS time, my friend and I both heard a faint little ceiling tap from the right side of the room.

"THAT'S how you do it!" I said, looking up toward the spot where the sound originated. Jeff was definitely getting the hang of things on the other side.

The Wolf Whisperer

Sally and Dick, dear friends of mine, owned two magnificent wolfdogs—Sasha, a beautiful black female with a saucy gait and inquisitive eyes, and Timber, an imposing gray male who looked like the perfect specimen Central Casting would send to a movie location. Timber wore his 16 years—112 wolfdog years—with a quiet dignity and unflagging devotion to his loving human pack.

Despite the fact a recent veterinarian blood panel showed him to have the constitution of a much younger wolf, Timber was having trouble navigating the stairs and I volunteered to do a Reiki session on the old boy.

Whit Neblett, who helps care for the wolfdogs, had told Timber I was coming to work with him. The afternoon I arrived, Timber crossed the garage floor to come to me, and pressed his massive head against my leg. I immediately sat right down on the floor and opened my arms. He gently stepped over my leg and let his once powerful body melt onto my lap. As I cradled him in my arms and visualized the healing Reiki symbols, I felt his muscles relax. My hands gently moved up his spine, feeling each sharp vertebra through Timber's thinning coat.

I opened my heart to this wise old soul, and silently asked him how I could best help him. He immediately began showing me pictures of him in his prime—racing over gently rolling hills in the moonlight, splashing in a shallow stream, rolling on his back in a meadow. His human parents later confirmed this was indeed the location of his previous home, when he was in robust health.

Now, however, he was letting me know he was ready to go. I continued to breathe slow, deep healing breaths, and Timber started to match my breathing. I could feel his link to the Earth gradually starting to fade.

"Jonna Rae! Don't walk him over yet!" Whit interrupted our soulful embrace. "Dick and Sally are leaving for D.C. for three days! He has to hang on until they get back!" With a thud, I felt Timber's spirit sink back into his body. He sighed deeply, as only an ancient wolf can. Then he slowly staggered to his feet, and stiffly walked away from me. I sent him my deepest heartfelt apologies.

Timber held on for his human parents to return from their trip, then reinforced his deep desire to be set free from his failing body by manifesting a hard knot of bone cancer on his left front leg. Emotionally devastated, the couple thanked him for 16 glorious years, and then released him to move on. He definitely took a big piece of their hearts with him in his journey to the stars.

But the wolf story continues….

White Wolf, Black Wolf

Knowing Sasha would deeply grieve the loss of her mate, Timber's thoughtful humans had arranged in advance to adopt another rescued wolfdog and bring him into the pack immediately.

I told Whit I'd seen Sasha playing with a white wolf in a vision. He and Dick had spent time with a beautiful alabaster male at Full Moon Farms, the outstanding wolfdog rescue facility in nearby Black Mountain in North Carolina. They both felt the animal could be a good fit. Juma had been abused by his previous owners, but showed the capacity to learn to trust and love again, and displayed no aggressive tendencies. He also had a reputation for being a formidable digger, and had a strong aversion to going anywhere NEAR a transportation cage.

Nancy, the owner of Full Moon Farms, was thrilled Dick and Sally wanted to adopt Juma. They'd found Sasha at Full Moon Farms years earlier, and Nancy saw how she thrived in her new home's atmosphere of love and respect. Nancy warned, though, that getting Juma into the cage was going to be a battle. It would take weeks to get him to the point where he would allow people to put a harness on him, she said, and even longer for him to be trained to a leash. And, of course there was the problem with him constantly digging. But then again, Nancy hadn't factored a Wolf Whisperer into the equation.

I accompanied Whit to the facility, and knelt by Juma's pen to talk with him while final adoption arrangements were made. As I have said, there's no "magic" about talking with animals—all you have to do is shift your consciousness from your analytical head into your compassionate heart. From that space of unconditional love, you first ask the animal for permission to connect, and then you start to project images and thoughts from your heart into theirs, and you also receive the images they decide to share with you.

First, I "told" the white wolfdog how beautiful he was. Then I mentally showed him pictures of the caring people waiting to welcome him into their pack, and the beautiful black wolfdog who would be mourning the loss of her beloved Timber. They all needed him in their lives, I told him. He would be safe, and loved, and honored, and respected. He would be able to run and play, and eat good food, and savor the quiet of the mountains in his own little kingdom. Juma took it all in. The delightful scenario I painted for him definitely got his attention.

When Nancy arrived to oversee Juma's departure, she and Whit carried the travel cage into Juma's pen.

"This is going to be a challenge," Nancy warned us. Then, to her shock, Juma immediately just stepped inside the cage and lay down while Whit quickly shut and locked the wire door. Whit looked at me and smiled, and I silently mouthed, "You're welcome!"

For the duration of our 30-minute trip back to Dick and Sally's home, I sat in the back of the van "talking" to Juma, giving him more images of the fantastic place he was going, telling him how easily he'd adapt to the harness and leash, and reminding him to keep "clean white paws on the ground" to prevent him from digging up the yard in his new home.

Another quick word here: When you want to relay a concept to an animal—or a human, for that matter—focus on the behavior or result you DO want, not the one you don't. For example, if I had been telling Juma, "Don't dig!"—the image I would have been sending him would have been of him digging hole after hole after hole. Focusing on the desired image of those clean white paws, resting calmly on solid grassy ground, reinforced the positive behavior I knew Juma's new family would want. I don't think he's dug a single hole to this day.

But back to Juma's arrival at his new home. Sally and Dick were brokenhearted at Timber's crossing, but smiled through their tears as Juma immediately bonded with them and Sasha. Because of the positive images we all continued to send him telepathically, Juma was wearing a harness in 24 hours of arriving at his new forever home, and walking on a leash within 72. Juma and Sasha romp through their five-acre enclosure as if they've been together for years, black and white, yin and yang. And, while no wolf could ever replace the magnificent Timber,

Juma is as patient, protective, and loving as Timber was throughout his long and happy life. The whole pack, human and wolfdog, is a vision of contentment and joy.

Dance of Discernment

I've mentioned in several previous stories how important I feel our dreams are. Here's one that I had shortly after talking with a friend about our personal interpretations of the Book of Revelations.

In the dream, my black Lab Bear and I were in a house that looked normal on a superficial level, but felt creepy. I was talking with a woman with short black hair. While I was listening to her words, I was also calibrating her energy, which was very dark.

"Think about it," she was saying to me. "Segregation is really a good thing. All people are NOT equal, of course, and it's important to keep them in their place...."

I strongly disagreed with her, but before I attempted to argue with her twisted logic, I pushed my awareness up higher to get a Christ Conscious reading of the entire situation. With this new clarity, I realized her eyes were completely black, and her skin was covered with scaly boils. The woman was a demon. There was a man in the room, too, and he was also a demon, with a thick fleshy tail protruding from his back.

The way dark forces are trying to win the war for our souls, I immediately understood, was to get us to turn against one another. If we can be seduced to sit in judgment on those who are different races, religions, economic status or any other fabricated criteria, we are chipping away at our humanity, our compassion, and our divine moral core.

Instead of willingly giving our power and our common sense to any individual or "cause," we must never lose a healthy skepticism, and we must always take full responsibility for our actions and our intent.

No matter how dark forces or fears twist our words and ideals, we have free will, and a conscience, and a natural ability to raise our consciousness to a higher state of divine awareness.

The dream wasn't about living in fear but rather living life as a constant dance of discernment. Evil is merely the absence of good. Darkness is merely the absence of light. Bringing compassion, patience, love, and light into a situation, or the world, can heal it.

As author, speaker and sage Gregg Braden urges us, use your power, and the gift of your life, wisely.

Claiming my Destiny

When I first learned which line on the hand represents "fame and fortune," I freaked. That line on my right hand is even more pronounced than my Life line, and blazes a strong trail directly up to my third finger, which represents "God-given gifts." Every palmist has confirmed, as did that psychic when I was 17, that I'm here this time to fully embrace my gifts of the spirit and guide others to discover their own natural abilities, too.

I "signed up" to help bring together the spiritual and the scientific, the psychic and the practical. The first step of that mission was living a relatively normal life and garnering credibility in the real world while actively utilizing my sixth sense. The second step was "coming out of the spiritual closet" to share my story and help make our natural intuitive ability completely mainstream. The catalyst for actually putting all this down on paper came in 2009, when I was contacted by a psychologist I didn't know.

"I hear you might be able to help a client of mine," she said. "I've been working with Cecilia for three years."

"What's her issue?" I asked.

"She sees dead people."

The fact that someone who was merely tapping into her natural ability was considered somehow in need of help broke my heart. The three of us met the following weekend, and the psychologist's client and I shared parallel stories, and immediately connected. She and I have become dear friends. She resisted going on psychotropic medications, despite the urging of her psychologist, because she didn't feel she was supposed to *blunt* her psychic ability, but rather to understand it so it no longer frightened her.

By today's harsh standards, Noah would have been on Lithium before he had a chance to drive a single nail into that first board. Joan of Arc would definitely have logged sanitarium time, as probably would other luminaries like Abraham Lincoln, who dreamt of his death 10 days before he was assassinated, or possibly even Bill Gates, who had a vision back in the 70s that computers could change people's lives.

The world's greatest painters, musicians, writers, scientists, religious and spiritual leaders, inventors, doctors—all of them are regularly tapping into this sixth sense that propels them into new dimensions of discovery, creativity, joy and connection.

You should be, too.

This isn't "New Age woo-woo." It's ancient wisdom. What's "new" about it is our fear to embrace it, and use it to enrich our daily lives, and the world.

For all the other Cecilias out there—people who are experiencing dimensions of awareness not everyone else has caught up with—this book is for you. There is **nothing** wrong with you.

Maybe, just maybe, by more of us coming out of the spiritual and psychic closet we can move the spiral of human consciousness up a few notches, particularly for the children who are coming into the world intuitively wide open. It's important for us to create a safe, nurturing environment for them to recognize and fully develop their abilities. They have cures to find, great art and literature to create, connections to discover and a whole world to heal. By tapping into "the Force," they will accomplish it all, and more.

To help you tune in to this part of yourself, the last chapter of this book offers "Om-Work"—10 proven tips to activate your Christ Consciousness state, in which you experience a Divine connection with all creation.

Coming soon—Practical Spirituality 101 Workbook

While the Om-Work is your crash course of touching into higher consciousness, the Practical Spirituality 101 class I was given in meditation 30 years ago takes you deeper, and gives you a bunch of resources to utilize while you're merrily traipsing through other dimensions.

This class, as the name implies, puts intuitive and spiritual practice into a "real world" format so you can immediately start using it in your everyday life.

Practical Spirituality 101 graduates include biogenetic researchers, psychotherapists, physicists, business consultants, environmental engineers, publishers, entrepreneurs, ministers, psychologists, lawyers, medical doctors, real estate brokers, artists, photographers, writers, social workers, and veterinarians, among others.

Besides teaching the class, I've been "told" in meditation and dreams to create a handbook that will walk people through the process, whether they're taking the class or just using the book as a "flight manual." That will be coming out in early 2011.

Big Spirits, Little Bodies©

Because kids are soooooo intuitively wide open, I've also been instructed to create both a class and a book specifically geared to young people. *Big Spirits, Little Bodies*© will reinforce the ability kids have naturally to "tune in." The book will also help their parents, teachers and other adults guide them effectively. Look for both the class and the book in 2011.

But right now, please turn the page and start your Om-Work!

Om-Work

Nurturing Your Inner Intuitive

So you're ready to embrace and utilize your own natural psychic abilities, but you're not sure where to begin? Here are the 10 tips I created to jump-start your journey.

1) When you get up, get UP!

A positive mind is an open mind. Set the tone first thing in the morning to shift consciously into a happy, receptive gear. When that alarm clock rings, it's the difference between saying, "Good God! Morning!" and "Good morning, God!" Try it and see. I KNOW it will work for you.

2) Journal your dreams and interesting occurrences.

When you're looking for something, you'll find it. In my Practical Spirituality 101 class, I tell students it's like suddenly deciding you want to buy a Subaru Forester. And, just as suddenly, you'll start seeing one Forester after another while you're driving. It's not that they magically started appearing out of thin air—they were always there. You just weren't being mindful of their existence.

In the same way, when you're looking actively and mindfully for divine coincidences that are outside the laws of probability, you're going to start seeing them. LOTS of them. And telling yourself you're going to remember and record your dreams means you'll actually start recalling the mountains of information you've been receiving in your nocturnal state.

3) Have an inter-species conversation.

Chat with your cat. Dialogue with your dog. Just move your consciousness out of your analytical mind and into your heart, where you're out of judgment. From that state of grace, where animals, plants and trees live, you can connect and communicate. Be respectful—ask them if they're interested in connecting first—and if you "feel" they're game, GO for it. Just because you might not have done it before only means you're ripe for trying it now.

4) Have an inter-dimensional conversation.

First, do the All-Purpose Affirmation—or any prayer that invokes a benevolent higher power and positive light—to put you in a safe mental and spiritual place. Then think of a loved one in the spirit world, and invite him or her to talk with you. Talk to a picture of the person, if that helps you focus your intent. Release any expectations for what you're about to hear from them, and just stay open. It might take a time or two before you're relaxed enough to connect. But, it's worth the extra effort when you start getting your proof that love never dies.

5) Laugh.

Life is supposed to be joyful. Laughter is the great equalizer—it dissolves barriers and brings people together. It heals. It invigorates. It rejuvenates. It burns calories, for petessake! There's even laughter yoga, which stretches the mind as well as the body. Where there is laughter, there is God. *Go* for it!

6) Listen/Meditate.

It's so easy for us to get stuck in our stories. Our "monkey brain" chatters incessantly, and we're distracted by bright shiny objects. It's only when we take a deep breath and mindfully become present in the stillness that we can really begin to open that inner door to our awareness. "Be still, and know that I am God…." Psalm 46:10.

7) Go outside and play.

Toss a ball, blow a bubble, make a snow angel, ride on a swing, wade in a creek, stare at a squirrel. Instead of "no child left behind," I want to start a "no child left indoors" movement. In nature, we become grounded and start to feel the rhythms of the Earth, and the Universe. That's when we begin to realize we carry the Universe inside of us. La la la la la!

8) Create something delightful.

Creative energy and intuitive energy come from the same place, that Christ Conscious state, or the Universal Field if you're a scientist. Create a picture in your mind of the thing you desire to create, whether it's a cake, or a kite, or a painting, or a sand castle, or a wonderful relationship. Then, breathe it into being through your hands and heart. As the divine creative energy flows through you, you're retuning yourself to flex your intuitive muscles, too.

9) Look for the lesson.

Nothing ever just "happens." Everything is part of everything else, and exists for a higher purpose. Our daily challenge is to cosmically "connect the dots," and see the bigger picture. When we start to push our brains to work a little harder to make these connections, the psychic part just happens. That's a promise, people!

10) Be thankful.

I feel the most powerful prayer we can say is "Thank you!" Push yourself to appreciate the beauty and value in the smallest things, and those small things become great things. Staying in an attitude of gratitude is more than a platitude. It's the bridge to a higher state of awareness and joy, and the state where you'll be living more and more as you continue to say a heart-felt "thank you!"

Thank YOU, too, for reading this memoir, and sharing my journey with me. My prayer for you is happiness—with yourself, with your life, with the limitless possibilities waiting for you to embrace them.

Reiki: An Ancient Art

By Jonna Rae Bartges

(Psychic Dimensions magazine; September 1978)

The totality of creation is imbued with universal life energy—swirling electrical masses of power waiting to be tapped into and focused. In this vast reservoir of strength rests the potential for the perfection of the human body, and the force that is the key to Reiki healing. The following is an exclusive interview with Virginia W. Samdahl, the first occidental to obtain the rank of Reiki Master in 2,500 years. Mrs. Samdahl was interviewed as she taught a class in Reiki healing at the National Southeastern Scientific Frontiers Fellowship Retreat at Guilford College in August of 1978.

For thousands of years, the Reiki method of natural healing was a mystery to the Western world. The secrets of the practice lay buried in the Sutras, forgotten even by the Zen Buddhist monks who once practiced the system.

Reiki (pronounced RAY-key), the Japanese words for Universal Life Energy, is transferred from master to student through the meditation and touch of the master. After the transfer, the student is then able to heal by gently placing his or her hands on the patient without altering the state of consciousness.

A master's touch kindles the Universal Life Energy, which lies dormant in every person and allows the healing force to pour through the student's hands and restore the body to its original perfect state.

So simple and efficient was the system that its Eastern practitioners eventually abandoned it, finding that Reiki given away made beggars of people. Once a person had been given perfect health through the touch of a Reiki healer, the person began to expect that the necessities of life would likewise be given to him, with no effort on his part. An exchange between the healer and the healee was necessary for the system to be truly effective. So, the monks, realizing that the world could not yet understand the law of exchange, abandoned Reiki.

It wasn't until the late 1800s that the system was rediscovered by Dr. Mikao Usui, president of the Christian University in Osaka, Japan. During a graduation, a student asked him why Christianity did not teach its ministers to heal. After all, every master who walked on Earth knew the secrets of restoring perfection. Usui couldn't answer, but the question spurred him on to an international search into the roots of every major religion to discover why the greatest schools of religious thought did not instruct students in the specifics of alleviating pain and suffering.

After years of intensive research and meditation, Usui rediscovered Reiki through a blinding flash of insight. As he ran down a mountainside after his sudden realization, he stubbed his toe and immediately healed it when he grasped his foot. Then he instantly healed a young girl's toothache by gently holding her face in his hands. And, his next miracle was healing a Bishop at a Zen temple after the holy man had suffered a gall bladder attack.

Drunk with joy of his new and powerful knowledge, Usui made the same mistake the monks centuries earlier had done— he began healing indiscriminately, never asking for an exchange. Usui was horrified to discover that after people were miraculously healed, they became beggars, just as the people had done in the time of the ancient monks.

But, instead of abandoning the Reiki method in this age, Usui carefully began selecting students and teaching them both the Reiki system and the necessity of an exchange between healer and patient. And, this time, Reiki began a slow but steady growth.

Meanwhile, in the United States, healers worked with spiritual and psychic disciplines to fill in the gaps left by orthodox medicine. Virginia W. Samdahl, a Park Forest, Illinois wife, mother, and active member of Grace United Protestant Church, was experimenting with healing through prayer. She found that whenever she was puzzling over a Bible verse, she would suddenly get "a super-duper wide screen production, like *Ben-Hur*, with all this stuff going on in Technicolor and hearing in my mind what was really meant by this passage. I thought it was pretty nifty; it never occurred to me that this was psychic."

With the help of some friends who gave her free reign in their metaphysical libraries, Mrs. Samdahl began developing her awareness and found that she was being drawn naturally in the direction of psychic healing. She wasn't always satisfied with the results.

"As I used and taught various healing methods, it was all very well to meditate and change your brain waves and get them down to 10.5 cycles per second so healing could take place and contact the mind of the healee and do all this stuff, and part of the time it was very effective. But, part of the time nothing happened, and I would blow wide open and say, "Why, why, WHY is nothing happening? Father, there's got to be a better way!'"

And, the better way began when Mrs. Samdahl met Reiki Master Takata. Then, in 1976, after three years of study and practice, Mrs. Samdahl became the first occidental to obtain the rank of Reiki Master in 2,500 years.

"Reiki is the most remarkable and most wonderful healing method I have ever encountered, and I have been in the healing ministry for many years," Mrs. Samdahl explains. "I can count on Reiki to work every time, and I cannot say that for any other healing method I've ever heard of, or used."

Perhaps the most unique aspect of the method is that the student learns to heal himself first, then members of his family, then others, in that order.

"I've seen healers who are in worse shape than the people they're trying to help," Mrs. Samdahl laughs. "That never happens with Reiki. Reiki healers are healthy, happy, wonderful people."

Since the revival of Reiki by Dr. Usui, there have been medical documentations of incredible healing through the gentle Reiki treatments. The principle behind the method is to heal the cause of the ailment, thereby eliminating the effect. Accident victims respond almost immediately to the touch of a Reiki Healer. Diabetes, blindness, heart ailments, allergic reactions, brain tumors, gall stones or high blood pressure are gradually healed through a series of treatments over a period of days, weeks or months. The treatments are effective even for patients who have absolutely no faith in the method.

The only cases where Reiki cannot be counted on to heal, says Mrs. Samdahl, are TB, hernias after age eight, and advanced stages of cancer.

"The pain of cancer can be reduced greatly or completely alleviated, but it must be caught in its early stages for the patient to have a total recovery," says Mrs. Samdahl.

Even with her many experiences of seeing a patient respond to Reiki before her very eyes, Mrs. Samdahl says that she has never gotten over the thrill of helping to restore a person's health.

"I believe that there is only one great Creative Force in the universe, which I call God," she said. "It is from this source that the Universal Life Energy is made available to us, for in order for us to be whole and to perform God's purpose for us here, we must be well. He has made this energy available to us, so we can be as He meant us to be; perfect in body, mind, and spirit.

"I never say that I will heal a person. I make it very clear that I am not doing anything—that God is doing it. But I do say that I feel the God power will help you, and hopefully, you might be healed."

An ordained minister with the Ministry of Christ Church, Mrs. Samdahl has had no trouble incorporating her practice of Reiki into her orthodox Protestant church.

"When I first got into the metaphysical movement about 15 years ago," she said, "I was so frustrated I was ready to leave our church. Then I decided to stop banging my head against the wall and start tunneling. And now when I hear these little pearls drop out of the mouths of my fellow parishioners, the same things I've been saying for years, I think, 'Ha! Gotcha!'"

"It's so important for me that I remain in my church and bring these concepts, which I consider to be truth, back to my church. For me, Reiki and orthodox religion go hand in hand. I won't consider myself a faith healer because according to some definitions, that takes a great deal of faith, either consciously or unconsciously, in the mind of the healer.

"I consider myself and all Reiki healers to be psychic healers. We heal with a power that we don't totally understand, and it doesn't take any faith. All we have to do is touch."

Mrs. Samdahl wonders if Jesus Christ might have been using Reiki since He, too, effected healing through a gentle touch.

"If we would realize our divinity, our ability would increase, knowing no bounds," she explains. "Christ realized His full divinity at the moment of birth, and we go to the grave refusing to admit ours. That's the main difference between Christ and us. Christ said, 'I am the light of the world, and you are the light of the world, so we are the same.' I never thought it was right that Christ was so far away. What good is He if you can never get to Him?

"People in my Methodist church where I was raised always had Him so far away. I think that's where we fall down in our healing ability no matter what method we're using; it's our lack of understanding of our own divinity. Of course, Christ had such a great ability because He was such a pure channel. All He had to do was reach out and touch."

Since Mrs. Samdahl became a master in 1976, three other Americans have studied and practiced to achieve that title. (**Note**: *Mrs. Takata initiated a total of 22 Reiki Masters during her lifetime.*)

Mrs. Samdahl holds classes the last week of each month at her home to initiate students into the first or second degree of the Reiki method.

After 15 people in an area decide to study Reiki and contact Mrs. Samdahl at her home in Park Forest, she travels to the region to conduct the class. She has initiated about 4,000 Reiki healers in two years, and hopes that thousands more will become interested in the method as word of Reiki spreads.

In accordance with the principle of a proper exchange, students are expected to pay $125 for their transfers and induction into the first degree. Immediately after a student receives the first of four transfers, he is able to direct the Reiki healing through his hands.

Although she is a very important New Age figure, bringing the ability to heal to thousands, Mrs. Samdahl remains humbled and candid about her role. She despised sickness and wanted to do something about it, she explains, and now that she's found the key, she shares her knowledge and her abilities with all who want to listen.

"Reiki is such a joy to use," she smiles. "I treat myself while I read or watch TV. The whole thing is really fun; it's such a zinger to see all of this stuff happen."

(In the 31 years since this article was published, millions of Reiki healers have been initiated all around the globe.)

A Physician's Perspective on End of Life Care

Paul's Care: A Physician's Perspective
By Michael Frederich, M.D.

May Bull (Paul's RN) and Julie Thomas (Paul's social worker) first discussed his case with me during a hospice interdisciplinary team meeting. As the weeks went by, it was clear to me that he and his wife Jonna Rae were exceptional people. I really wasn't surprised when Julie and May requested a home visit by me both in the role of team physician for pain and symptom management and as chair of the hospice ethics committee to discuss options for his end-of-life care.

It was obvious on my first encounter that this gentleman's disease was progressing rapidly. The right side of his face had been largely destroyed by his melanoma, yet his spirit and determination were evident from my first encounter. We discussed his options and his desire to not die as his father had—with life-prolonging interventions he did not desire. We discussed controlled sedation as an option to assure his comfort should his symptoms and suffering become refractory to other less intense interventions. He made it clear to me that when he felt the time was right he would forego prophylactic antibiotics which were keeping him from becoming septic and would also not wish artificial hydration and nutrition. After recommending a hydromorphone (Dilaudid) subcutaneous infusion to help manage his pain, Paul seemed more relaxed knowing that he had options about the end his life would take.

Paul did very well for a considerable length of time after this meeting, until the episode where his hand was caught in his wound and he decided to forego antibiotics and artificial hydration and nutrition while being admitted to the hospice inpatient center for controlled sedation. His admission was as described by Jonna Rae.

Because San Diego Hospice had used sedation on other patients prior to Paul's admission, I was surprised by the reaction of the nurse who refused to increase his versed infusion. At the de-briefing later, the main objection was that Paul had walked into the inpatient unit under his own power. We learned from this that the physician needed to remain at the bedside, increasing the infusion until the patient was comfortably sedated, and reassuring the nursing staff that all was well. We in fact changed our procedure after this case.

Paul developed full-blown sepsis on the second day of his sedation with his face becoming quite dark and gangrenous. His fever reached 105 degrees F. He remained comfortable on anti-pyretics and his hydromorphone until his death as described by Jonna Rae.

Among the incredible things about Paul was the many legacies he left us. His spirit was invincible, and he certainly impacted many things at Disneyland. The world of hospice and palliative medicine also owes him a debt. As a result of this case, I became more aware of potential perceived problems with sedation as an ethical modality. When I became chairman of the AAHPM's ethics special interest group, I led the effort to write and have adopted the following position statement on Sedation at the End of Life. I hope it will help others like Paul have access to this appropriate modality:

AAHPM Statement on Sedation at the End-of-Life
Approved by the Board of Directors
September 13, 2002

The American Academy of Hospice and Palliative Medicine regards sedation as a valid, ethically sound, and effective modality for relieving symptoms and suffering in some patients

reaching the ends of their lives. Sedation is reserved for those in whom suffering is refractory and is not ameliorated by the application of other appropriate palliative care measures. These appropriate palliative care measures may include but are not limited to pain relief, non-pain symptom management, mental health care, and spiritual counseling.

As one of the many forms of palliative treatment, the use of sedating medications is intended to decrease the patient's level of consciousness to mitigate the experience of suffering, but not to hasten the end of his or her life. Since this represents both an intention and an outcome that is beneficial, sedation in these cases is ethically justified. It is not analogous to euthanasia or physician-assisted suicide in which the primary intent is the death of the patient.

Careful patient and family assessment is a critical part of the evaluation process before sedation is provided for any individual. Hospice and palliative care programs and healthcare providers should undertake a thorough assessment of the alternative treatments available and engage in an open interdisciplinary decision-making process. This process must include the patient, if able, and family or other appropriate surrogate decision-makers, if the patient lacks decision-making capacity, in order to assure informed consent. Rarely, in emergent situations, sedation may need to be applied prior to the appropriate discussions. In these cases, the discussions should take place as soon as possible once the comfort of the patient has been ensured.

Patients for whom sedation may be appropriate are most often near death as a result of an underlying disease process. Although the withdrawal of artificial hydration and nutrition commonly accompanies sedation, the decision to provide, withdraw, or withhold such treatments is separate from the decision whether or not to provide sedation.

Michael Frederich, M.D., is regional medical Director for Trinity Care Hospice in Torrance, CA, and has been involved as a hospice medical director for 23 years. He is trained in medical ethics and, as chairman of the ethics special interest group of the AAHPM authored the AAHPM Position Statement on Sedation at the End of Life. Frederich recently received the NHPCO and NCHPP 2004 Heart of Hospice Award in the Clinical Caregiver category.

(Reprinted with permission of National Hospice and Palliative Care Organization from INSIGHTS magazine, Issue Two, 2004)

The Real Cecilia

When Jonna Rae asked me if she could include my name and my story in her book, I immediately said, "Of course— and I want to write something, too!"

It's important to me that you know everything she wrote about me (page 208-209) is true.

I'm an intelligent woman. I have a Master's Degree in Education, I've taught for years, and I implement special programs in schools to help both students and their parents get the most out of the educational system.

When my psychologist contacted Jonna Rae and the three of us met, it was so comforting to talk with another person who didn't try to deny there are other dimensions of awareness, and when we lose the fear and look for the deeper meaning, we can truly begin living our lives more richly.

Meeting Jonna Rae it was a big confirmation that we didn't come here by accident, we each came here with a purpose that is uniquely our own.

I am learning to understand that the best validation that I can have is my own. Because I am a teacher, I like to transmit to my students that we all came here with a sensitivity that we can grow and use in a powerful, positive way; we just don't do it on the same day or by the same method.

I know what I have is real, and being friends with Jonna Rae is helping me to be OK with who I am. She's helped me understand that we are beings of love and light. When the power of love is bigger than anything, life happens…and it's healthy, compassionate and beautiful.

Thank you Jonna Rae for sharing all this and for helping me to not just be real, but the real me.

About the Author

Clairvoyant and clairaudient since childhood, Jonna Rae grew up seeing glowing spirit "visitors" in her family's circa-1750 Pennsylvania farmhouse. By the time she was in her early 20s, she knew she had to find out once and for all if she was "psychic" or "psychotic."

She resigned her position as a national editor at the Allentown Morning Call newspaper and embarked on what would turn out to be a two-year spiritual quest.

A highlight of her work was doing psychic readings for Peter Caddy, co-founder of the Findhorn Foundation, and his infant son during a visit Caddy made to Miami in 1984. Caddy invited her to be the resident psychic at his Mt. Shasta community in northern California. Feeling the timing wasn't quite right, she respectfully declined.

Jonna Rae is a spiritual counselor and minister director with the Universal Brotherhood Movement, Inc., a Reiki Master and a Deeksha Oneness Blessing Giver. She is a proud descendant of the Wolf Clan of the Leni-Lenape Tribe of the Algonquin Nation. Visit her Web site at www.happymedium.us, and contact her at jonnarae@happymedium.us